Through the Grief

A Mother's Journey

Dayton Ann Williams

To order additional copies of this book, contact:
Xlibris Corporation
1-888-795-4274
www.Xlibris.com
Orders@Xlibris.com
73477

To my son, Tyrell, who made my heart smile. While I deeply miss him, I celebrate his freedom as he soars on the wings of the eagles.

Semper Fi

contents

acknowledgements

Paula Kuether who encouraged and supported me in sharing my story, for reviewing the manuscript, and for the inspiration she continuously provides.

Bonnie Miller and David Harris provided their friendship and support during my journey, and reviewed the manuscript's first draft.

Susan Henry Photography for the skill and compassion, Susan H, Susan, and Jennifer provided in creating the cover photos.

Robert Ferguson, Bonnie Miller, Caleb Williams and Hope Williams for their review of the cover photos.

The United States Marine Corps, and the Marines of the 1/2 WPNS Co 81's Platoon who served with Tyrell, for their boundless support and the honor they bestowed upon my son.

Ed Davis provided his unconditional love; never-ending support; and the honor of being able to call him my dad.

My dear friends walked with me on my journey and extended their support and love as only they could.

forward

This story describes a chapter in my life; the heartrending death of my eldest son, Tyrell Seth Williams. Tyrell was killed in a hit-and-run accident on 11 February 2008 in Austin, Texas approximately 6 weeks after his 31st birthday and less than three months of an honorary discharge from the United States Marine Corps. The person responsible remains unidentified.

When I heard the news the following morning, this chapter of my life began. To date it is the most devastating and heart-wrenching experience that I have had. Tyrell served three tours in Iraq and when he returned home from his final tour I was able to finally breathe freely. My son was now safe. At the time I did not consider, nor could I fathom, the possibility that Tyrell's time with us was limited. Tyrell was no longer in harm's way and the possibility of death was no longer a constant companion.

While journaling has been both healing and growth enhancing for many years, I found myself recoiling from pen and paper during the bereavement process. Each time I wrote, I released a flood of tears and my body responded with a dissonance that seemed to assault every cell in my body. Consequently, some of my words are from memories that may be distorted from the passage of time. My intent is to speak from my heart, and in truth, to reveal the journey for what it was: a path laden with pain, depression, remorse, joy, love, and healing.

With the support of my father, my friends, my children and even strangers, I have found comfort and help along the way. Through my personal relationship with spirit, I have discovered a depth to my soul that I did not know existed and a path to healing that was supported and encompassed by love.

As humans, we unequivocally know that we will die. We hear about death every day through the media and, at times, from those with whom we have a personal relationship. Nevertheless, we often erect a wall of separation between what is happening to others and deny the fact that this, too, will happen to us.

It is when death touches us personally that we are open to the reality that surrounds us every day. In that moment, we empathize with every man, woman and child who has lost a child, parent, spouse or friend. We grieve for them as we grieve for our self; and mourn the loss of everyone who has gone before us.

At this point death becomes our teacher and allows us to experience our humanity in ways we previously could not grasp. Death, who was once our foe, ultimately becomes our friend as we move through our journey of healing. We begin to understand, at the very core of our being, that life is fleeting and each *moment* is to be savored as if it were our last breath.

May these words offer comfort to those who are suffering with a recent loss and support in knowing that you are not alone. Please know that it is both loving and healing to be gentle with ourselves.

DAYTON WILLIAMS

As you travel your path, hold fast. You will heal, you will rekindle your passion for life, and your heart will smile again.

From my heart to yours,

Dayton

> *The memory of the dead is placed in the life of the living.*
> —*Ciscero*

prologue

This is a story of a human experience; the tragic and untimely death of my eldest son. It is a story of glorious accomplishments and numerous foibles. For a mother, it is an experience that is so horrific we do not want to contemplate, or even attempt to imagine. The very idea appears to go against nature as a mother should not outlive her child. Nevertheless, countless people throughout history have experienced this very tragedy.

A mother is emotionally wired to put her child first. Experiencing the death of a child will force one to look in a different direction and from a different perspective. This can be very disconcerting, and cause much pain, for we are in a state of confusion without knowing what to think or how to feel. All of the ideas and scenarios that defined us have radically changed, or no longer exist. The ensuing journey spans months and years where the soul seems caught in the netherworld, yet life continues all around us.

In actuality it is a chapter in the story of my life. Each of us has a story and it is the summation of the chapters that provide the totality of our story. We are not defined by the chapters of our lives, however, the chapters do define our experiences. How we respond to our experiences becomes woven into our psyche and ultimately becomes part of our story. I visualize our stories to be akin to a patchwork quilt: multiple colors with a variety of patterns, shapes and sizes. If you are like me, you would prefer that your life represented a beautiful tapestry. One that is pleasing to the eye and presents a stunningly picturesque country scene or a beautiful room filled with elegant furnishings and serene inhabitants.

Life, however, is meant to be experienced in its entirety, and this means that we will have beautiful and blissful moments as well as sad and painful moments. It is the truly painful moments that help us to savor the truly splendid moments. It is great loss that allows us to feel great love.

At times I wish it were different. I wish life was *easier*. At these times, I am aware of the petulant child within who stamps her foot and screams 'it's not fair!' I smile for I must agree that it is not always *fair*. Yet it is life, and I have chosen to be fully engaged; at least most of the time. It is when we are engaged that we are awake to all the possibilities, and all the miracles, that surround us. This is, by far, the best possible place to be.

DAYTON WILLIAMS

For many years I fled life. While I momentarily eased my pain, I poisoned my body, mind and spirit. I emotionally harmed those around me as well. The price of attempting to control my environment was beyond my ability to pay, and beyond what my soul and psyche could endure.

While I can unequivocally say that it was not fair that my son was taken in this tragic and senseless manner, how I respond to what happened will create beauty or ugliness in this chapter of my story; this section of my patchwork quilt. I am, always, responsible for the choices that I make.

My story actually begins a few months earlier in the summer of 2007. I was on an international assignment for my company and had been living and working in Stockholm, Sweden since early 2005. As I had fallen in love with the country, and the Scandinavian people and culture, I wanted to move there permanently. I had received a job offer and was in final negotiations.

On one of my home trips in June, I saw my doctor for the yearly physical. It was a Monday evening in mid-July when I received the results in the mail. I opened the envelope and was completely unprepared for the document that I held in my hand: cancerous; biopsy to be scheduled immediately. Once the initial shock dissipated, my next thought was clear. *If* it was the worst case scenario, and I was gravely ill, I did not want to be 5,000 miles from my children. I did not want to spend the remainder of my time on this earth with that much distance between us.

It was at that moment my decision was made. I was returning to the US. While I knew it to be the best decision, given the information that I had, I was deeply sad to be leaving the country and people that had captured my heart. On my next home-trip I completed the biopsy. The biopsy was negative for cancer and from a medical perspective I was completely healthy.

While the results sunk into my consciousness, I was both relieved and saddened. My decision to leave Sweden had been based upon a premise that was no longer valid. I would be returning to the US with a broken heart and shattered dream. In looking back, I am deeply grateful for the outcome. By returning to the US, I was able to spend several magnificent weeks with my son before he departed this earth.

> *Trust thyself.*
> —*Ralph Waldo Emerson*

DAYTON WILLIAMS

the first two weeks

In many ways, this was the easiest part of the journey. As Tyrell's death was sudden, there was an enormous amount of preparation and a multitude of decisions to make; and all was to be accomplished in a very short time. The sheer magnitude of tasks propelled me forward and kept me in motion. Since I could focus on the immediate task at hand, it was often a shield to the devastating pain that was rotting my soul. Two things were of utmost importance: how I best honor my son, and how I provide support to my children.

Shae and Caleb had suffered an overwhelming loss; and it broke my heart when I thought how difficult it would be for them to learn to live without their brother by their side. They were all close and the void would create a chasm so wide that it would be difficult to learn how to cross it. What I did during these next few weeks would remain with me for the rest of my life, and this was ultimately my driving force.

After I received the call, I was paralyzed for a period of time. I could not align my thoughts and my emotions. There was a part of me that could not believe it was true; that did not want to believe it was true. I called Tyrell's cell and it went to voicemail. This did not convince me, however, and my mind struggled to find a way to prove that my son was not dead; that a terrible, terrible mistake had been made.

As I pondered the possibilities of how I could end this nightmare and find my son alive and well, it occurred to me that I needed to call my manager. It was early afternoon on a Tuesday and the day had begun as a typical workday. I can only imagine what it was like for her to receive the call. I was on the verge of hysteria, my sentences were choppy, and my voice warbled uncontrollably. I found it difficult to breathe. I told her that my son was killed, I had to log off, and I had no idea when I would be back. I could feel her kindness as she gently spoke to me and told me how sorry she was and to not worry about work. I was free to focus on what was important; making the arrangements for my son.

I recall making three other telephone calls: my father, Mark, and the detective handling Tyrell's case. I eventually reached my dad on his mobile and asked if he was able to talk. I relayed the news and felt his strength support me through the distance. I then called Mark. Mark is a dear and long-time friend and I needed his help in passing the word. It would be impossible for me to call everyone and I knew that Mark would help in getting the word to our friends and colleagues. The outpouring of mail and calls that I received was testament to Mark successfully fulfilling my request. I was unable to reach the detective and was referred to the police counselor that I would meet the following day.

The lack of information regarding the accident was disturbing. As the months passed, and the details remained sparse and sketchy, I would wrestle with the absurdity and incomprehensibility of my son's life ending with virtually no information as to what happened, or who was responsible. At the conclusion of our discussion, I received details regarding where Tyrell's body was held and prepared myself for the next call.

My hands trembled as I dialed the telephone number of the coroner's office. The woman I spoke to was kind but emphatic in her response to my question, "How do you know it is my son? He could have lost his wallet, which someone picked up, and became the victim of this tragic accident", I heard myself saying. As I listened to myself I nearly laughed at the absurdity yet cried because I wanted it to be true!

This was my first encounter with the dichotomy of grief; the opposing contradictions of the logic and the emotion. Through the ensuing days, weeks, and months I would become very familiar with the experience and was grateful when I recognized that I was not losing my mind to madness. Grief simply had a life of its own.

She assured me that the identity was unmistakable; that it was Tyrell Seth Williams. I asked when his body could be released and she replied they were ready to release him. She asked if I had identified a funeral home and my tension escalated. I had no idea what my next step was until she said funeral home. I became manic as I thought of Tyrell lying in a freezer in the coroner's office. For some reason it made my stomach twist into a thousand knots and I decided that I had to get him out of there. The visual was simply too much to bear. With this focus, my role of mother took flight and I was in motion.

Since I lived two hours away, the only option available to me was the internet. I pulled up my typical search engine and typed in funeral homes + Austin, TX. Within moments I had a plethora of options available to me. Whenever I am searching for a service provider, I read through all of the options, return to the beginning, and stop when I *feel* it is right. But, this was not one of my normal searches, and I was having difficulty concentrating and feeling anything but the agonizing pain that assaulted my soul.

I became impatient and began to feel the panic swelling within. I took several deep breaths and returned to my search. My eyes fell on Weed-Corley-Fish Funeral Home and I clicked on the link. I spent a few moments reading through their site and knew this was the perfect choice. It turned out to be a g*od deal.*

God deal is the term that I use to describe a situation that, without any effort on my part, turns out to be the perfect scenario. It is always laced with the extraordinary and wrapped with perfection. It is when everything falls into place, and I am able to observe the magic of creative love. There were to be an abundance of god deals in the ensuing weeks and months. Each one gave witness to the miraculous and evoked deep gratitude.

I placed the call to the funeral home and explained my circumstances; it was necessary to retrieve Tyrell's body from the coroner's office that afternoon. The gentle voice explained that I would be required to sign a release form, and they would need to receive it within the next 30 minutes in order to meet the deadline. He emailed me the form, which I immediately printed and completed all the fields. I attempted to fax it back; however, I only received error messages. I began to panic as I could not figure out what was wrong with the machine.

It was Lopez who intervened and volunteered to get the document faxed. I could feel myself shaking with relief. Later that afternoon I received a call from the funeral home. They successfully retrieved Tyrell's body, and they would take very good care of him. I sat and wept for a long time. This was only the beginning.

On Wednesday I would drive to Austin to meet with the funeral director. I was grateful, and concerned, when Caleb told me that he was going with me. Caleb was in the midst of a challenging semester at the university and I did not want this to impact him. The responsibility was mine to go; not his. He was adamant and I accepted his support. We left early Wednesday morning for Austin.

While Caleb's friends were at the house within hours providing support, Shae's friends were also doing the same for her. It is a tremendous blessing that my children have such wonderful friends. They were constant companions and supporters through this period, and I know how much it meant to both of them. While Caleb and I drove to Austin, Shae and her friends occupied the *command post*. Caleb and I would contact them whenever we had questions, or required assistance.

Our first stop in Austin was the funeral home. We had to pick up Tyrell's belongings so that we could get the key to his house and truck. We retrieved the paper sack and rushed to Tyrell's home where we were to meet the Austin Police Department Counselor. When I entered Tyrell's house, I felt a wave of anxiety wash over me. I called out his name; hoping that he would respond, and I would see him walk through his bedroom door with sleepy eyes and his usual smile.

The house was eerily quiet and as I walked through I saw representations of the man that he had become. His bed was made. The sink held only a couple of items. The house was clean and organized, and the board on the wall of his office listed tasks and due dates. Tyrell had made this his home, and he was thriving. I was still struggling with the thought of the immense tragedy. Everything that he had worked for was now destroyed. The tasks on the board would forever remain undone.

The police counselor arrived and while I was anxious to get to the scene of the accident, he had another agenda. It was his job to ascertain the emotional state of both of us and ensure that we understood avenues of assistance that were available to us. We finally concluded our conversation and climbed into his car for the drive to the scene. Although I was told that the accident occurred approximately a mile from Tyrell's home, it seemed that we were driving forever. Later I learned that there was a much more direct route.

As we drove into the parking lot, I noticed Tyrell's truck. It remained where he had parked it Monday evening. All of the times that I had communicated *don't drink and drive* seemed to flood into my consciousness. I realized that those words had directly resulted in him walking home from the sports bar; had directly placed him in harm's way. With my heart pounding at the realization, and tears forming in my eyes, I exited the car and requested to be taken to the exact location where Tyrell was struck; where he took his last breath.

As I walked across the parking lot and onto the street, I could feel my chest tightening and my breath constricting. I saw the markers in the street and knelt down. As my hand moved across the concrete, and finally rested upon the stain from the blood of my son, I felt an anger rise up that was so fierce I feared it would utterly consume me. At that moment, I hated the person that took my son's life. At that moment, I wanted them to suffer as my son had suffered. At that moment, I was lost.

The fury would stay with me for the next 24 hours, and then I released it. I simply did not have the energy to maintain that level of intense emotion. Nor did I want to put my energy into hate. What energy I had was required to help my children, and myself, get through this. I would not allow my focus to be diverted to something that was outside of my power; a focus that took me away from Tyrell. These next few days were to be centered on how we would say good-bye; how we would celebrate the time that Tyrell was with us.

I looked around and found some coins and picked them up. I noticed a rock, picked that up as well, and placed everything in my pocket. These tokens would be added to my tray which held special stones that I had acquired over the years. A car appeared, as it careened around the bend, and I was pulled aside. I looked around and noticed a camera on top of the storage units across the street. It was pointing directly at the spot that Tyrell was struck.

I felt a gleam of hope as the tape would provide the entire event and the person would be identified. I called the number and was placed on hold for what seemed to be hours. Finally I heard a man's voice asking how he could help. I blurted out the situation and told him that I wanted to speak with the manager. I was placed on hold again and after awhile I simply hung up. I later learned that the police checked into the situation and the camera was completely for *show*. It had never been activated.

Tommy and Eric stopped by the scene of the accident; it was wonderful to see them. After we visited awhile, Caleb and I returned to the funeral home to discuss the arrangements. We were to have a 3-way call with Shae and Russ, the children's father, so that everyone could have input into the arrangements. I was very pleased with how well the planning session went. We secured consensus on each and every activity and I was confident that everyone was comfortable with the decisions. It was perfect.

To see us come together and support one another in this way was exactly what I wanted. And since we were so close, it was exactly what I expected. I was confident that we would get through this and support one another along the way. Reality would prove to be quite different than what I envisioned.

Since we would not return to Austin until the viewing on Saturday, Caleb and I had to return to Tyrell's home in north Austin to secure his dress uniform. It was late in the day and we would need to hurry. As we were driving, I attempted to reach Neill. Neill and Tyrell had been friends since grade school and Tyrell was thrilled that they were once again living in the same city. My heart ached as I relayed the news to Neill; I knew his loss would be great. He conveyed his support, and requested that I let him know if he could help in any way. I was grateful that Tyrell had experienced such wonderful friendships along his journey.

Once we reached Tyrell's house, we entered with trepidation. The possibility that this was a mistake, that this was not real, was now destroyed. We were here to gather the clothes for Tyrell's last presence with us. As the reality sank in, we walked to Tyrell's closet and began pulling out the trunks that held his military paraphernalia. As neither Caleb nor I knew exactly what was required to complete the dress uniform, we identified everything that could possibly be used. We found duplicates of medals and placed them all in a bag. We were running out of time and needed to return to south Austin.

Once we gathered everything together, we were on the road again. We reached the funeral home shortly before closing and raced inside. I was apologetic and explained that we did not know exactly what to bring, and asked them to let me know if they required anything else. The gentleman tenderly took my son's possessions and said they would take care of everything; he was confident that we had provided exactly what they needed. As I looked into his kind eyes, I began to release a flood of tears. I whispered my deepest thanks and turned to leave.

Caleb and I walked outside and stood for a moment while we caught our breath. Although it had been an exceedingly stressful day, we had completed our mission and accomplished everything that we needed to do. It was now time to return to Bryan and stop somewhere along the way for dinner. I had deprived my son of food all day; it was time that he received some nourishment.

Thursday proved to be another packed day. My first task was to go to the Verizon Wireless store. I had been anxious to get Tyrell's phone so that I could call all of his friends. I knew that if Tyrell had someone's number listed in his phone, then that meant they were important to him. When I received the sack from the funeral home, I quickly opened it looking for the phone. To my horror the phone was in several pieces. Even though there was nothing to indicate it was salvageable, I pressed the button to turn it on. Nothing.

My heart sank and I could feel my eyes fill with tears. The thought of not being able to contact his friends sent a spasm from my brain to my stomach. I thought I would be physically ill. It was with apprehension that I entered the store and walked up to the customer service counter.

As I relayed my situation, I heard my voice cracking and knew, at any moment, the anxiety would escalate to the point that I would have difficulty speaking. The woman hearing my story said there was nothing that she could do. I was astounded. In our digital age it would appear anything was possible. I asked if she could speak with technical services and she agreed to make the call.

DAYTON WILLIAMS

As she turned to leave, one of her colleagues asked what the trouble was. She explained the situation and he said that he would try to recover the data. While he was heads down working on the phone, I found myself speaking to the manager. Since the phone was not in my name, I had no legal rights to the data. I pulled out my Power of Attorney that Tyrell had given me when he was deployed. Since the date was still valid, she was willing to investigate and determine if it was an acceptable document.

While waiting for a verdict on whether the data could be recovered, and whether the information would even be given to me, I closed my eyes and took several deep breaths. I had done everything that I could. It was now time to trust. Several minutes passed and the manager returned. The Power of Attorney was acceptable. I breathed a sigh of relief and continued to wait.

Approximately ten minutes later the gentleman returned. He was able to retrieve the data and transferred it to the phone which he was offering to me while he spoke. He assured me everything was there. They helped me reset the password so that I could listen to any voicemails. I felt immense relief wash over me. I thanked them for their willingness to help me, and indicated that I could return the phone in approximately two weeks. As I left the store I released a *thank you* as I breathed.

Thursday and Friday were consumed with phone calls and emails. I began by listing, in a notebook since I did not trust my memory, all of the people listed in the address book on Tyrell's mobile. I made notes as I called each one: left a message; temporarily not in service; wrong number; comments from the ones that I reached. I regretted having to relay the devastating news over a telephone line: for myself and for them.

After I completed all of the calls, I responded to the voice mails: a job interview; an appointment with the VA clinic; an appointment with a VA counselor. While each call made was excruciating, my next task of hacking into my son's email accounts invoked extreme dread.

I knew that I would be able to reach more of Tyrell's friends via his email accounts. While the logic was sound, the idea was distressing; it was a complete violation of my son's privacy. The fact that I knew that he was no longer with us did nothing to silence my intense feelings. This was not a normal situation, and I was not operating at my normal efficiency.

Each task produced a dichotomy; what I needed to do, and revulsion for having to do it. Every time I took a step into Tyrell's private world I acknowledged his death, and I did not *want* to do either. But it was necessary. These were Tyrell's friends and many were his Marine brothers; those that he served with and they supported one another through horrors that most of us cannot imagine. They had a right to know what became of their *brother*, and they needed to hear it from me.

With the help of Shae and Caleb providing probable passwords, I was eventually able to get into all of Tyrell's accounts. I added the list of names to my notebook and began to send emails. As with the phone calls, I received an outpouring of support.

One particular response was a healing balm to my broken heart; it was from Major Laube. He was currently stationed in Germany and unable to make the services however he took the time to write a long mail and shared multiple anecdotes of my son. I forwarded the mail to the family, as I knew they would appreciate it as much as I did. It was wonderful to hear so many details of Tyrell, and from someone who extended so much honor and respect.

The obituary draft was due to the funeral home by noon on Thursday, as was our decision as to whether the viewing would include an open casket. Shae was handling the obituary, as this was something that was very important to her. After a couple of revisions and discussions, the final document was submitted in time. The funeral home would be responsible for submitting the obituary to the Austin Statesman, and I submitted the obituaries to the Bryan/ College Station Eagle, and the Daily Oklahoman.

Tyrell was born in Oklahoma City, and his father and grandfather still resided there. Bryan/College Station was Tyrell's home prior to entering the Marines. Since none of the services were to be held in Bryan, I wanted to ensure that his friends, whom I was unable to reach, would have the opportunity to receive the news.

With the decision communicated that we wanted an open casket for the viewing, the remaining tasks in preparation for the viewing were to submit pictures for the DVD and information for the memorial. Shae and I discussed the pictures and she submitted all information required by the designated time.

Having completed the calls and emails to Tyrell's friends, I took some time for basic housekeeping tasks: submitting change of address for Tyrell's mail; changing the utilities to my name; contacting the VA and setting up an appointment; cancelling cable and satellite services; contacting the Dallas/Fort Worth National Cemetery to discuss arrangements; contacting my manager to get details regarding my bereavement leave. By Friday evening I had accomplished a great deal. I took some time to simply rest before my daughter arrived. Saturday would be a challenging and emotional day for everyone.

We left Bryan early Saturday morning for the trip to Austin. The farewell and viewing would begin at 3:00p and we needed a couple of hours to prepare for the gathering that would take place afterwards at Tyrell's home. On the way into Austin, I asked that we make a detour to the mini-mart where Tyrell and I had stopped on our first house hunting trip.

This action of wanting *to connect* would stay with me for some time. As we stood at the counter to pay for our purchases, the clerk was having challenges ringing up the items. The register continuously blurted out *uh oh*. It became quite comical and the clerk had all of us laughing before he finally figured out how to make it stop. I exited the mart with a feeling of gratitude for that simple exchange had lightened my heart.

Shae and Caleb dropped me off at Tyrell's house and went on to the store to pick up refreshments for the gathering. Very little was required to prepare the house. I washed the dishes, and picked up the bins that Caleb and I had strewn all over Tyrell's bedroom when we looked for his dress uniform the previous Wednesday. After I had everything in order, I began to walk through the house and reminisce; it was merely six weeks prior when I helped Tyrell move in.

I took the responsibility of cleaning the house while Tyrell drove all over Austin picking up his furniture and other items. By the end of the day we were both exhausted, however, he wore a brilliant smile on his face. He was thrilled to be in Austin, and to be in the house. I looked around the rooms, at the color scheme, and wished that I had gone ahead and painted it when he had moved in. The colors were atrocious and he was so supportive in helping me save on expenses that he was willing to wait a bit before he painted.

Standing in the house, and gazing at the walls, I realized that I would have to paint before I put the house on the market. A pang surged through my heart at the lost opportunity to have given Tyrell the simple pleasure of freshly painted walls. I was extremely fortunate to have Stephen Sunshine as my realtor; for the purchase as well as the resale. A consummate professional, his help was immeasurable and I remain deeply grateful for all the support that he provided.

In due time, Shae and Caleb returned and I was able to set my remorse aside, for the moment, and we did what we could to prepare for the gathering. The children's father and uncle stopped by, and we all left for the funeral home.

It had begun to lightly rain and this comforted me. It seemed as if the angels were weeping with us as we gathered to say farewell to the man who was a son, a brother, and a friend. It was Caleb and Shae who first saw Tyrell. They went in together and I was deeply grateful to witness how they supported one another. Before others arrived, Russ went into see his son and to say goodbye.

Several of Tyrell's and Caleb's mutual friends arrived from Bryan and Austin, as well as friends of Tyrell's from Austin. The room that was set up for the viewing was beautifully arranged and the DVD that they had created was deeply moving. They had set up the viewing room off to the side which provided a separation from the sitting area. I considered this to be an expression of immeasurable compassion. It provided the necessary balance in order to process the feelings of saying good-bye, for the final time, to the physical form of someone that was deeply loved.

A woman, whom I had never met, entered the sitting area and approached me. She introduced herself as Laurie and said that she was there on behalf of our company, my manager, my friends, and that she, too, was a Marine mom. A mutual friend and colleague, Bob, had contacted her as she lived in Austin. I was deeply grateful for her presence, and for the love and concern of my friends who would not be able to make the gatherings due to the great distance. Laurie was a genuinely lovely woman and through her hugs, and the compassion that I saw in her eyes, my heart received much comfort.

After a period of time, it appeared that no one else would arrive and it was nearing the allotted time. I spoke to the children about beginning the gathering at Tyrell's a bit early. It was agreed that Caleb would take everyone to the house, and Shae would stay with me while I spent some time with Tyrell. I was grateful for my daughter's support as I sat outside the viewing room and watched the video. Once it concluded, I walked inside and looked around. My eyes fell upon my son, as he laid in the coffin to my right. The gasp that exploded from my mouth held such force that I felt my knees go weak and my arms reach for something to steady myself.

Once I could move, I advanced to my son. I was struck by the look of serenity, and the faint smile that creased his face. I began to speak to him and allowed myself the freedom to express everything that was in my heart. Time seemed to stand still as I gazed upon my son for the final time. When I felt ready, and had said everything that I needed to express, I left the room and returned to my daughter. We then spent some time together with Tyrell before we drove to the gathering and joined everyone.

Having the last gathering in Tyrell's house was very important to me. This was the city that he had chosen to begin his life and this was the house that he had made his home. We spent the next couple of hours eating, drinking, and sharing stories of Tyrell with joy and laughter. The atmosphere was positively charged with memories of my son and I knew that this was exactly what he would have wanted.

As the gathering concluded, Shae, Caleb and I remained. The next few hours would be very challenging for my children for I had tasked them to determine what possessions they would take for themselves. As I would not return to the house for several weeks, I wanted to remove the items that were of significant value. I watched Shae and Caleb move through Tyrell's possessions and was deeply touched by the respect that they exhibited; to one another and to Tyrell. After the decisions had been made, we loaded the car. As I locked the door, and turned to leave, I felt the tears on my cheek as I reflected on the memory of my beloved son.

On the drive to Bryan, I was the navigator. I had *thought* that I could easily reverse the directions and successfully return us home. However, I was relatively new at the bereavement process and had not yet figured out the degree of dysfunction of my brain to responses. I missed the exit from the toll road and we drove a very long time before we could figure out what to do. The situation evoked our own version of an Aggie joke: How many Aggies does it take to drive from Austin to Bryan/College Station? Apparently it was more than three because that was how many we had in the car, and we were lost. This amused us for some time and we finally recognized a familiar street as we regained our course and completed the drive home.

Sunday was spent with my children. I remain immensely grateful for this day, for we would never gather again in this manner. Part of the day was spent finding the song that contained a message for us. It was a labor of love as Caleb and Shae worked together. Finally it was discovered: Modest Mouse *Float On.* As we sat on the couch, looking at the lyrics and listening to the words, we gently cried together. This was Tyrell's song for us, and we were grateful for the gift.

Tyrell had sold his car shortly before his death, and I had received a call the previous week from the new owner. They had found his dog tags. Shae and Caleb went to pick them up and when they returned Caleb handed them to me. I placed them around my neck where they remain until my vow is completed.

DAYTON WILLIAMS

While Shae was working on her computer and scanning in photos in preparation of the celebration, she received an email from my aunt. My aunt, and her family, did not support the organization that we had chosen for a memorial; they wanted, instead, to send money to the soldiers that Tyrell served with.

As Shae was relaying the message, my agitation was increasing exponentially. What, in the world, was my aunt talking about? The organization only used rescued dogs and they provided the hearing and balance dogs at no cost to the recipient. What was there not to support? It was the epitome of an organization who provided a valuable service to those in need. Furthermore, they were not soldiers; they were Marines. I was so appalled by my aunt's message that I did what any grown woman would do; I called my daddy and tattled.

As I relayed my extreme frustration to my dad, I was also aware of how disconnected I felt from myself. It was as if the past decades of my life melted away and I was once again a frightened little girl. All I wanted was someone to simply take care of me: to hold me; wipe the tears from my face; and tell me that I would be ok. I told my dad how horrible my family was because no one had called, or sent a card, or attended the viewing yet, my aunt sends a callous message that reeked of disrespect and dishonor.

My dad was extremely patient as he listened to me rant. After I released my emotions, I slumped back on the couch and waited for my dad to speak. He gently told me not to be concerned, and to keep my focus on Tyrell, Shae and Caleb. He would take care of my aunt. I was grateful for my dad's support as it allowed me to release my frustration, return to the present, and continue to enjoy the day with my children.

Decisions decreased somewhat during the week before the celebration and funeral. My meeting with Cynthia at the VA office was invaluable in understanding the various actions that I needed to take, and I was immensely grateful for her compassion and support at this early stage of my journey. The funeral director called to inform me that Tyrell's cremation was completed. The words seemed to move through a vast sea and once they reached my ears they were distorted and garbled beyond recognition.

It was the difficulty of wrapping logic around emotion that was so challenging. My mind understood and accepted the necessity of the situation, however, my emotions were appalled with the implications. I simply had to sit in a daze for awhile until it passed. Fighting the feelings was senseless, and denying they existed was perilous to my psyche. Consequently, the only remaining option was to simply *feel the feelings*.

I received a call from 1st Sgt McDonald and was delighted to hear from him. He informed me that he would be presenting me with the flag during the ceremony, and that he and his wife would see everyone at the celebration.

Caleb and I went shopping for a suit. The funeral would most assuredly be hard on him. At the very least I felt he would be more comfortable if he was able to dress for the occasion. The smile on his face, when he tried on the suits, assured me that my decision was sound.

DAYTON WILLIAMS

In Dallas, Shae and her friends were busy with preparations for the celebration. Shae arranged for a van, and Tony offered to drive the family members that would be attending the funeral. Tony picked up the cigars, and Amanda and Shannon went grocery shopping. Shae continued to scan hundreds of pictures as she prepared for the display that would continuously run on two separate televisions, and Tracie helped with activities. The celebration would begin on Sunday morning, and conclude with the funeral and gathering on Monday. I remain deeply grateful for everyone who worked so hard to make it a glorious event.

It was also during this week that Caleb and I began a daily routine of watching a *How I Met Your Mother* episode. Shae had loaned the DVDs and we found this simple ritual to be extremely therapeutic. The ability to sit for 30 minutes with no purpose except to respond with laughter to a funny situation or comment was wonderful. Once we completed Season One, I purchased Season Two. Once we completed Season Two, we went through the entire series of *The Vicar of Dibley*. By the time we had completed series, our need to continue the ritual had passed. It had served its purpose by helping us experience the emotion of joy, which brought balance to the grief bursts that were a component of our daily lives.

On Saturday morning, Caleb and I began our trek to Dallas via Austin. Our first stop was the funeral home where we picked up Tyrell's urn, his cover, the memorials and the remaining items from the viewing. I remain deeply grateful for everyone at Weed-Corley-Fish Funeral Home, and everything that they did to produce a beautiful memorial to my son. To experience their care, compassion, and support during such a difficult time was a tremendous blessing to all of us.

Once again we made the drive to Tyrell's house. Tom was to meet us to pick up the treadmill and the Harley. The Harley was not operational. Mike had graciously offered to get it running, and Tom graciously offered to get it to him. We picked up the mail and the cable box, and dropped off the cable box as we left Austin.

The cable store was located off of Mopac, and just a little south of the street where Tyrell was killed. As we drove past the exit, I glanced to my left. My eyes fell on the sports bar and I felt the magnitude of my loss. I placed my hand on the urn, and silently expressed how deeply I missed my son. By Saturday afternoon, weary from the trip and the day's activities, we arrived in Dallas.

Sunday proved to be everything that I had hoped and dreamed. It was a magnificent day of celebrating the life of my son. We started at 9:00a and continued the entire day with narratives of Tyrell, pictures, food, drink, cigars and laughter. Friends of Tyrell, Shae and Caleb arrived along with the children's father, their uncles and wives, and my dad and his wife, Joanne. My friend Susan stopped by for a bit, and my friend Jeff, on behalf of my friends and colleagues, made the trip from Phoenix. The focus was on honoring Tyrell and I felt extremely blessed to be part of the experience, and honored that so many wonderful people stopped by to celebrate with us.

I had difficulty expressing myself, as I was in a state of permanent sensory overload. This was to be the first of future experiences in which I moved in a manner that I was not accustomed to. I wanted to have an opportunity to visit with everyone and struggled with completing my desire. I was especially distressed by not spending more time with the 1st Sgt and his wife. His presence was very important to me, and I regretted the missed opportunity.

I was also saddened that I had not spent more time with my dad and Joanne. Outside of my children, my father and Joanne was my sole support from my family. I loved them for this, and for being there for me during this unspeakable loss.

I had lost *myself* and communicating in a group was something that I struggled with for many months. It was one of many changes that I would experience as a result of the bereavement process. It was as if I had to relearn how to be a social being: how to connect with others; how to connect with myself. While I noticed this radical change in myself, others did not notice, or were merely understanding and extending kindness to me. While it distressed me at a personal level, it did not obstruct the gratitude that I held in my heart for the day that was reserved for remembering and honoring Tyrell's life.

Monday, 25 February 2008. The day for placing my son's cremated remains in their final resting place: a niche in the columbarium at the Dallas-Fort Worth National Cemetery. As I dressed for the services, I reflected on the past 14 days. A mere two weeks had passed since my son took his last breath. It seemed like an eternity, and yet it seemed like only a moment had passed. Shae would drive Caleb, their father and me. Tony would drive the Williams' family members and my dad and Joanne. I was becoming anxious as we were nearing the time that we needed to leave, and folks were still scurrying about. I considered taking a cab; it would certainly decrease my stress and prevent unnecessary and sideways anger being released. I felt, however, that it was important to stay with my children and dismissed the idea.

As we drove to the cemetery, I became increasingly tense and scolded myself for not taking the cab. The children were with their father and they would have been fine. These thoughts stayed with me until we arrived. I immediately exited the car and told my daughter that I was going for a walk.

I walked across the grounds and reached a columbarium. I squatted down, sat on my heels, and read the names before me: so many people; so much loss. My heart wrenched for all the parents, spouses, siblings and friends that had gone before me; those that had placed their beloved's remains in a niche, and experienced the same sorrow that was now coursing through my body. I sent a blessing of healing and release for us all.

As I walked back to the car, I met the gentleman who assisted with the services. He explained that we would follow in a procession up to the ceremony. I thanked him and sat down to rest a moment. Tom approached me and sat beside me. I spoke with him a bit, happy that he was with us, and noticed a man approaching across the lawn. I stood and walked towards him. It was Vaniel. I had not seen him since I left Boulder and learned that he, and his family, now lived in the area. Vaniel was always an inspiration to me, and I was deeply touched that he would come to offer his support and condolences.

It was now time to begin the ceremony. As we walked up to the pavilion, I noticed the Color Guard was all Marines. I felt a gasp escape as I understood what an immense honor this was. I knew that 1st Sgt McDonald had created this magnificent gift, and my heart was profoundly moved. As I sat at the front, my focus never left the Marines that stood before me and to the side. As they moved through the ceremony, their dignity and precision was glorious to behold. I was grateful that my father had expressed his desire for Tyrell to be interred at a National Cemetery. Had he not told me his wishes, this would never have transpired.

Once 1st Sgt McDonald received the flag, he turned to approach me. As he knelt before me, and spoke the words that have been uttered thousands of times to women across our land, I felt Tyrell's presence; I felt my heart smile. As I received the flag, the joy and grief collided within me and exploded in a symphony of gratitude for the man, and friend of my son, who knelt before me. As he stood to leave, I clutched the gift that was a representation of my son's service to our nation.

I cherish the memory. There was no greater way to honor my son's passing from this world. My father wanted to protect the precious flag that I held, and would later present me with a case so that it would be preserved and displayed. I treasure the gift for I am forever reminded of the magnificent ceremony and the honor bestowed upon my son.

After a period of silence, the gentleman approached the front and announced that the service was concluded. The family would move to the columbarium. I began to feel panic swelling within. I was disoriented and did not know what to do. I had thought that I would have time to visit with everyone and thank them for coming. No one had thought to hand out the memorials so there would be many people who did not know that we would gather at Shae's house afterwards. This distressed me greatly and continues to deliver a twinge of remorse when I think about it.

I also wanted to thank the Color Guard and 1st Sgt McDonald. I located him standing next to the Color Guard and ran towards him. I told him that I wanted to thank the Marines and he promised that he would pass along my gratitude. I asked if he would join us at the columbarium, and he replied that it was for the family only. I assured him that he was a part of our family and he graciously accepted.

As we gathered at the columbarium, I held the urn and uttered a few words before I turned to place my son's ashes gently in the niche. I watched as the workers sealed it, and placed the temporary marker that would identify the place of internment until the permanent marker was received. We turned and walked to our cars and would meet again at the gathering. As I walked, I sent a blessing to everyone who participated in this day; whether in the flesh or not. It was each action, each presence, each thought, each prayer that culminated into this glorious ceremony. Gratitude filled my heart and became a soothing balm across the ocean of grief.

Once we arrived at Shae's home, I was immediately encompassed by the love that filled the air. Friends and family members were there to provide their support, and the afternoon continued with a celebration of Tyrell's life. As I moved through the living room,

I noticed three young men and a young woman that I did not know. I asked Shae and Caleb if they knew them; they did not. I approached them and learned that the young men were Marines; they had served with my son.

I was ecstatic to meet them and expressed my deepest thanks for making the ceremony and attending our gathering. Their presence meant the world to me; and I expressed that they were our honored guests. Without knowing anyone they came solely to give tribute to Tyrell, and this deeply touched me. Chris and Kirby had traveled all the way from Florida, and Joshua and Meghan lived in the area.

The rest of the day was spent with these wonderful people. We heard numerous anecdotes and received insights into many of the photos that Tyrell had in his collection. It was truly a delightful afternoon, and the presence of these young Marines was a gift beyond measure.

It was difficult to end the day, and I would have loved to have continued the celebration indefinitely. However, Caleb and I had a long trip back to Bryan and we needed to get on the road. As we bade good-bye to everyone and drove away, I felt immensely grateful for the outcome of these past two weeks. While there were numerous challenges, and painful incidences, there were many more experiences of love, healing and expressions of honor to my son. Knowing this brought comfort, and would continue to bring comfort over the months ahead. It was now time to begin the journey of rebuilding and reaffirming life.

But now faith, hope, love, abide these three; but the greatest of these is love.
I Corinthians 13:13

probate court

It was 10 June 2008 and the appointed day to attend Probate Court. While this was something I had been striving to attain for months, it now became a source of trepidation. As my court appointment was at 9:30, I would need to leave the house by 6:30a to ensure that I made it in time. Technically, it really did not have anything to do with making it in time. It was more of a matter of ensuring that I had plenty of time for the *unknowns*. It had been a long time since I drove in Austin's rush hour traffic and I simply do not know what to expect.

I am driving my Mini because I want to relieve yet another stress; parallel parking in front of the court house. It is amazing what the mind focuses on. In order to divert attention from anything unpleasant it will latch on to the most bizarre thoughts. While I have not parallel parked in a *while*, it was certainly something achievable. To cease the massive debate within my mind I acquiesced to the fact that I would drive the Mini. The debate ended.

I slept fretfully and was up before 5:00a. No concerns with getting out the door by 6:30a. The drive into Austin was without incident. Often I observed that I was the only vehicle, and attempted to focus on how wonderful it felt to be on the road; enjoying the scenery and the drive. About 30 minutes outside Austin the traffic exploded into a parking lot with hundreds of shapes and colors. After the same light turned green five times before I was able to cross to the other side, the stress began to build and I took deep breaths to calm myself.

As I approached I35, I was reassured; I was nearing my destination. When 30 minutes passed, and I had only advanced eight miles, I began to calm myself with more deep breathing exercises. I still had time and that was the main thing to concentrate on. Why waste energy when it was not necessary? It was going to be a challenging day as it was; no need to intentionally create chaos.

I finally reached my destination and drove around the block a couple of times to locate a meter. I discovered a meter and hopped out of my car with the $5.00 worth of change that I had secured from the mini-mart where I stopped on my way in. I plugged in two dimes before I noticed that the meter was non-functional. How could that be possible? The only parking around the court house was metered therefore all meters ought to be fully functional. I returned to my car, threw the change in my lap, and proceeded to search for another spot. As I had already been around the block a few times previously, I would need to extend my search area if I had any hopes of securing a legitimate spot.

I was several blocks from the court house, but I located two spots. I pulled straight into the spot, sprang from the car, and ran to the meter. It, too, was not working! I began to craft a letter in my head that I would send to the mayor informing him of the necessity of ensuring all meters within a 2 mile radius of the court house must be in working order at all times. This was so important that a special task force needed to be assigned. I walked to the adjoining meter and discovered it was a functional meter. In seconds I was back in my car and pulled up the appropriate amount to ensure that my vehicle was within the painted white lines.

Once I reached the meter I learned that the maximum limit was 2 hours. I proceeded to plug quarters into the slot until I saw the flashing number 2. I raced to the court house as it was 9:00a and I had wanted to be in the building by this time. I was close so I rejected the notion that I *needed* to panic and began walking as quickly as my narrow heels would allow. I often wondered why *certain* shoes go with a *certain* outfit. And why do suits require heels? Once again I pondered these questions as I quickly approached my destination.

I entered the 2nd floor and did not see anything that even remotely resembled a court room. I approached the young woman at the nearest desk and asked for directions. She informed me that I was in the wrong building; the court house was diagonally across the street. Apparently my face contorted to an expression exhibiting intense horror and another woman in the room offered to help. I thanked her repeatedly and followed directly behind her as if she was a hen and I was her little chicken.

When we reached the front door she pointed to the court house and I turned to express, once again, my gratitude. I raced to the street light and waited impatiently for the signal to grant permission to cross the street. Upon entering the court house I quickly placed my belongings in the scanner and waited for the hand signal instructing me to enter the doorway that was suspended before me. I cleared security and darted for the elevators that would take me to the 2nd floor. As the doors opened, I glanced at my watch. 9:15. I allowed a deep release of breath; I had made it. Now it was time to wait for my attorney.

I had never met my attorney. He was filling in for my *real* attorney who resided in Ft Worth. As the probate must be held in Austin, given this was where Tyrell was domiciled, my attorney had secured the assistance of a local attorney to attend the proceedings in his stead. A young man approached me and I noticed the cowboy boots. A small smile begins to crease the corners of my mouth as I thought *only in Texas*. He asked if I was Dayton Williams and I extended my hand in greeting.

My attorney moved to the desk at the end of the hall and informed the clerk that we were present for our hearing. We then located a place to sit and he took me through the various scenarios of what would happen once we stood before the judge; reviewing the questions that would be presented. While the questions were simple, I found my mind struggling to respond. I began to weep and a pang of sorrow filled my heart. I did not want to be here. I did not want to stand before strangers and discuss my son; to acknowledge that he was dead.

There was something fundamentally wrong with the entire setting. I had a moment where I considered running madly down the halls; and out the door of the court house. Instead, I stood up and began pacing; all the while apologizing to my attorney. I actually thought that I would not *break* until I stood before the judge. Once again I found that my emotions had their own agenda and they expressed themselves in whatever way they chose; regardless of the appropriateness of the time or place. I had come to learn that it was in my best interest to literally *go with the flow*.

I completed the review with my attorney and the court appointed attorney ad litem approached. She introduced herself and informed me that she needed to ask a few questions. I had already developed an opinion of her after I was told how she *interrogated* the witnesses that we identified. While on one hand I knew that she was just doing her job, I also believed that it could have been done in a less aggressive manner. There are approximately 6 questions that were asked of the witnesses. Spending 30 minutes to ask the same 6 questions in dozens of different ways became tedious and wore on everyone. Nevertheless, that is what transpired and what was going through my mind as we shook hands.

She told me that she spoke with the children's father the previous evening to ensure that he agreed with me being named the Administrator of the Estate. Thankfully he did, or we would have had a serious problem. The whole reason we were all gathered at the court was to have me legally identified as the administrator. It seemed a little late to be asking anyone if it was *okay*. She then asked how I *knew* Tyrell did not have a will. I then relayed the last conversation that Tyrell and I had on Sunday evening, 10 February, about 26 hours before he took his last breath.

Tyrell had attended an introductory seminar regarding selling attorney services. He was explaining the opportunity and asking me for feedback. One of the services provided was wills and I stated that the cost of a will alone was worth the fee that a customer would pay. We spent another 10 minutes discussing wills and why they were necessary. He acknowledged that he wished he had created a will when he had the opportunity to do so, and while he was still in the Corps.

I smiled and told him that would have been ideal, however, creating a will at his earliest opportunity was the next best thing. As I shared this conversation with the attorney ad litem, she responded with "how interesting that we would have this conversation the day before he was killed". I told her that there had been dozens of these types of scenarios; where things just *fell into place*. The clerk called the case, and as we concluded our conversation, we stood and walked into the courtroom.

There were two proceedings ahead of mine and I took a moment to take in my surroundings. All of these people were here because they had experienced a loss. For a moment I was overtaken with grief: theirs and mine. I turned to the attorney ad litem and handed her the second news clipping regarding my son. She read it and as she returned it I noticed her eyes had clouded with tears. I accepted the paper and sent a thank you to the universe. In that moment, through the healing power of compassion, I was able to release the frustration that I had previously held.

Nearly 45 minutes passed before we were called before the judge. As I began to weep as soon as I reached the bench, the first order of business was to locate tissues. After a moment the judge began to speak, and I waited until questions were directed to me. Both attorneys moved through the process with ease. There was something to be said of experience; it certainly provided efficiency in getting through a task, and more so when the task was not altogether pleasant.

The proceedings concluded and the judge handed the appropriate documents to the clerk. The next step was to file them with the court office; and receive authorized copies identifying me as the Administrator to the Estate of Tyrell Seth Williams. I paid the $10 fee, shook my attorney's hand and quickly exited the building. At that moment, the only thing I wanted to do was get outside; stand in the sun; and breathe deeply.

After I secured a sufficient amount of oxygen so that I could easily return to motion, I began to look around and determine my bearings. Where did I park my car? My mind began to retrace my steps, however, it had not been operating at optimal capacity for several months. Anything that required any degree of concentration took significantly more time than previously. I despised it although I had learned to live with it. I walked a block before I realized that I was going in the wrong direction. I made a u-turn and within short order I was sitting in my car.

I now had a dilemma. I had taken a day's vacation to go to Probate Court and the central task that I wanted to accomplish was to make it to the Title Office and transfer Tyrell's Harley to Shae and the F150 to Caleb. This was my mission and, therefore, I was intensely focused on getting this completed. However, I also wanted to go to Dripping Springs and meet Sheri and her Texas Hearing and Service Dogs staff. It was late morning and I had time to stop by the facility and still get to the Title Company before it closed. I reminded myself that this, too, was important to me. After I became weary of the chatter inside my head, I pulled out the directions to the facility, turned the key in the ignition, and pulled out of the parking space.

As I exited the facility, I reflected on how delighted I was in choosing to visit. Sheri and her staff were absolutely wonderful. I was given a tour of the kennels, and had an opportunity to watch them at work. As I began the 2.5 hour trip back to Bryan, I was aware of the gratitude bursting from my heart.

Securing the transfer of titles went without incident and it was about half past 4. I decided that I would stop by Hospice to see if I could speak with Joan. Fortunately she was available and, as always, I enjoyed the opportunity to spend some time with her.

My next stop was the UPS store. I was sending Shae's tag and title overnight. This really was not necessary, however I was so excited to be able to bequeath the Harley that I wanted her to receive the ownership papers as fast as possible. I had one more task and that was to give Caleb the title to the Ford. I walked quickly to my car and started it up.

Fortunately Caleb was home and I asked him if he had a few moments. As we sat in the living room, and I expressed how happy I was to present him, on behalf of Tyrell, the title to the truck. He graciously accepted it; and I was grateful that he had allowed me the opportunity to turn over the title *in my own way*. Since the truck was now his, we went to check it out.

As we looked around the cab, Caleb was familiarizing himself with *what does what*. After some time he pushed the button activating the recorder, and Tyrell's voice boomed through the air. I began laughing and crying, was happy and sad, all at the same time. It was so wonderful to hear his voice, and so fitting to hear it at this particular event; the transfer of title to his little brother. This was indeed a day of celebration.

The greatest degree of inner tranquility comes from the development of love and compassion. The more we care for the happiness of others, the greater is our own sense of well being.
—Tenzin Gyatso, the 14th Dalai Lama

DAYTON WILLIAMS

work

P rior to Tyrell's death, the only constant in my life, besides my children and friends, was my work. My work defined me and it gave me purpose. Instead of working to live, I lived to work. It was while I lived and worked in Sweden that I began to see the devastation that I had brought upon myself by allowing my work to consume me. This was one of the gifts that my Scandinavian colleagues and friends gave me. I witnessed and experienced what *living* was all about.

It was during my time in Sweden that I began to limit the number of hours that I would work each week. Once I returned to the States, and took a gig where I traveled to San Francisco every week, it was not long before I returned to my old habits. I was tremendously discouraged.

The week of Tyrell's death I was to have flown to San Francisco, however, I cancelled my plans the previous Thursday and observed myself sitting at my desk crying uncontrollably. I did not know what to do. If I had been ill or hurt I would have taken myself to the emergency room. However, I did not know what to do with the overwhelming feelings of despair. I wondered if I was losing my mind. I called my company's mental health hotline and secured an appointment on Monday, 11 February 2008, at 7:00p with a counselor. It was a mere 3.5 hours later that my son would take his last breath on this earth.

Obviously issues with my work took a backseat when I learned that my son was killed. I was granted two weeks of bereavement leave and returned to work two days after the burial of my son. When I logged on to my email, I learned that I had been released from my project. At the time, I was devastated for I had just lost my son. Was I to lose my job as well?

It took a couple of days to figure everything out and I was transferred to a new project where I have been since March 2008. These past months have brought a wide range of emotions in relation to my work. I have had the privilege of having two managers, Dani and Pam, who offered enormous support along the way. Additionally, I had the opportunity to work with Jim, one of the best executives that I have known during my time with the company. I have friends and colleagues whom I deeply treasure, and am extremely grateful for the opportunity to have such wonderful people in my life.

I have also had some of the worst experiences during these past months. It was to the point that I knew it was time for me to leave the company. However, I also knew that I could not make any changes in my life till after the first year. My focus needed to be on healing. I doubt that I could have made any decisions anyway; most of the time I was on automatic which amounted to merely taking the next step in front of me.

By nature, I am an action person. However, during this period the challenge of taking an action was often analogous to walking through quicksand. Each action produced an opposite reaction to my intent. One day I decided to do something that I had not considered in the past, I added Theodore Roosevelt's quote to my email closing: *"In any situation the best thing you can do is the right thing; the worst thing you can do is nothing."* While I did not witness a radical change in my colleagues, and a rallying together as a Team to support the account, I felt better. I had communicated what I considered essential; and it was a step for me in learning how to return to myself.

Working was often the only thing that I did consistently during the bereavement process. Since I worked from home, I did not have to shower or get dressed to begin my work day. And there were many, many days that I did neither.

Because I have such a stressful job, most of my energy went to just *doing* my job. The remaining energy was directed at taking care of Tyrell's estate. Anything else was accomplished only if I had any remaining energy; and that was rare. In looking back I do not know if it was a blessing or bane that I worked from home. I suspect it was like most things in our lives; it was a little bit of both.

On the one hand, since grief takes on its own life force, whenever the grief flooded through me I could stop and take some moments to shed tears until it passed. On the other hand, I was completely isolated from others. Since my first gig back to the US resulted in flying to the West coast every week, it did not lend time for cultivating friendships and participating in social activities. Consequently, I did not have any friends in the town that I lived.

It was the isolation from life that proved to have the largest impact on me. I thrive when I connect with others and it became challenging to connect in a virtual environment. Everything that I had previously done to be successful was becoming difficult to sustain. Partly it was merely that I did not have the passion, patience or energy that I once had. Partly it was simply the effects of a deep loss.

I am grateful, though, that I had my work; it was important to learn how to move forward and a daily routine of work was conducive for that purpose. Finding meaning and purpose in life would occur over time, and after a period of time, so maintaining my work was one of the few activities that I had that was familiar and comfortable.

It was during the year anniversary of my son's death that I began to secure a clearer picture of the changes that I would make regarding my work. I had decided that I would take a day's vacation and drive to my son's resting place. A couple of weeks prior I became incapacitated with a painful back and was on short-term disability for about three and a half weeks. Consequently, a six hour round-trip was completely out of the question. I was appalled that I had allowed myself to become so stressed at work that I acquired this condition.

While I could not change the situation, it was a catalyst for change and I began to actively seek a permanent solution.

I also began participating in volunteer activities during this period. It offered me an opportunity to get out of the house, and to offer something to others. I had learned long ago that if I am feeling *blue*, the best cure is to pick up the phone and call someone and ask them how they are doing. In other words, get out of myself. While it is an excellent activity, it must be balanced. There is a difference between grieving and being stuck in grief. While the first is natural and necessary, the second can be detrimental.

Getting outside oneself is helpful if one is stuck in grief. During my bereavement process I would hear from others who experienced this life changing tragedy; the loss of their child. Some took years before they ever left the house. Some memorialized their child whereas 10 years or more had passed and it was as if the event had just happened.

Finding a way to engage in life without centering on one's loss is a heart-wrenching challenge. Hopefully we can find comfort in knowing that regardless of the circumstance, if we are open and our desire is to seek balance, our journey will take us to a state of peace. And, this is the gift.

Examine who you are, why you exist and what you believe. Then make a commitment to aligning your work and your spirit.
—Russ Jones

relationships

I began this section with a box of tissues by my side. Depending on how long it takes me to complete, I may have to make a trip to the store before I can continue. Perhaps I ought to have planned better and not begun this section without at least three boxes of tissues. Then again, perhaps I am simply afraid because this is the topic that has caused me great sorrow during my journey. This is the area where I often failed to come from a place of love. This is an area that highlighted my shortcomings. I consider it a sign of health that I am making the attempt to write, and am reminded of the slogan *progress not perfection*.

Our journey is simply that; *our* journey. Yet our journey will, without fail, cross and interconnect with others along the way. In each of these crossings, our goal is to understand the gift extended by the relationship and ultimately accept it. Those we meet will stay for the period of time that fulfills our need, and theirs. Some will stay for a short while, others longer. To be able to celebrate the relationship, rather than focus on the length of time, brings the greatest joy. For this is when we are truly in the present moment; this is where creation exists.

I believe that family is important; our friends are dear; and those that challenge us the most often become our greatest teachers. How we respond to our relationships do not define who we are, rather they reveal the areas that are opportunities for healing. While I sit in my home, without interfacing with another soul, I am a relatively happy and carefree person. I am supportive, loving, and kind. This is how I define myself and since there is no one to state otherwise, I can be self-assured of my assessment.

Yet, by only being with myself, and by myself, I have not revealed anything regarding who I really am. It is when I venture outside myself, and into the world, that I discover an interconnection with all things. It is where I discover the areas within that are in the greatest need of healing. It is where I become aware of the occasions that I am not so supportive; not so loving; and not so kind. It is my relationship and interactions with others that help me ultimately heal.

While deeply challenging, it is essential that those who have suffered a traumatic loss open themselves to the support of others. This support may come in the form of individual counseling, a support group, time with a priest, pastor, rabbi or guide, or it may involve a mixture of these avenues. We may also be fortunate to find help through friends or family members.

Our inner guide will direct us to those that will support us. It is only a matter of opening to the experience; of allowing ourselves to be vulnerable. As the grief darkly colored my perceptions, I often had difficulty *hearing* my inner guide. It was at these times that I could only press on and while a particular person, or group, may prove not to be the right *fit*, the mere fact that I continued to move forward would guarantee success in due time.

I did not have a positive experience with the support group that I encountered. It was a group specifically for parents who had lost a child; consequently, I thought it would be the perfect fit. As this organization spans across the country, I am confident that they provide enormous value to many people. It just was not the group for me.

I did have a very positive experience through a clinical psychologist, Dr. Stagner, and have continued weekly sessions; although the focus has shifted and includes discussing work and other areas. This is an indication that I am moving forward, and moving in the right direction.

I also had the opportunity to spend time with Joan Serber, Hospice Brazos Valley Bereavement Coordinator. Joan was truly an angel of mercy and I am thankful for her compassion and support. Hospice is a wonderful contributor to communities, as their bereavement support groups are open to anyone who has suffered a loss.

I remain forever grateful to my friends, across the US and Scandinavia, who reached out to me; and was there for me, when I reached out to them. Each brought me a gift that was wrapped

DAYTON WILLIAMS

in love and contained comfort and hope. Each gave from their heart and in a way that only they could offer. It was their love and compassion that assisted me in my healing. Though words may fail me in expressing my thanks, my heart continues to beat with the constant reminder of their love.

Paula, who has been my spiritual guide and mentor for many, many years, was my anchor in the storm that ravaged my soul. Her limitless and steadfast love offered support and guidance, which was crucial in helping me maintain perspective as I moved through the bereavement process. She was, and continues to be, a tremendous blessing. It is my hope that she receives ten-fold that which she so freely gives to others.

I experienced a change that I became acutely aware of after the first month or so, and it was a considerable time before I regained myself. My tolerance level had dramatically decreased to where it was often nonexistent. I simply did not have the energy, or the desire, to play games, become involved in office politics, placate *stupid* ideas, or enter into senseless and meaningless dialogue. My entire world had been destroyed and succumbing to petty and trivial pursuits seemed pointless and a complete waste of time. Needless to say, there were implications in interacting with others when I came from this perspective.

The one thing that still brings a pang to my heart was hearing the tragic news of my son's death from my daughter. The fact that her father called her instead of me was, from my perspective, inexcusable. The fact that she felt she ought to be the one to tell me was heartbreaking.

My daughter phoned me and asked if I was able to take some time to talk. She wanted to make sure that I was not on a conference call or in the middle of something with work. She also asked if I was sitting down because she had some very sad news. I actually *smiled* in hearing her words because I knew that I could handle anything she was experiencing. Smiled; the thought still sends a chill down my spine. When she relayed that Tyrell had been killed, my mind and heart exploded and I discovered myself on the floor screaming and wailing. Caleb rushed into my office and asked me what was wrong. I merely handed him the phone which forced my daughter to tell Caleb as well.

This was the first time, in decades, that I had not been present for my children; and it was a time when they needed me the most. This single event tainted the weeks and months that followed. In many ways it has continued to impact my relationship with my daughter as it became a breeding ground for other issues. Since I cannot go back in time and relive that moment, the only option available to me is to move forward; and trust that healing will come to us all.

A situation arose that caught me completely off-guard and proved to be devastating for myself and for my children. It involved family dynamics that I had been separated from for more than 20 years. That it would arise after all this time never occurred to me; nor was I prepared for my response.

The event surrounded a conversation regarding clearing Tyrell's belongings out of his house so that I could put it on the market for sale. I had just purchased the house the previous December and Tyrell had only been in the house for about 6 weeks. I considered

DAYTON WILLIAMS

keeping it, but it was simply too painful of a reminder. Consequently, I needed to get it on the market as quickly as possible to reduce the expense of having an empty house. I had envisioned that Shae, Caleb and I would make the trip and clear out the house. At the last minute Shae extended an offer to her father to help, and he accepted. This caused me extreme grief and the multiple conversations between Shae, Caleb and I resulted in hurt feelings across the board.

I finally decided that the only way I could endure a weekend of removing Tyrell's possessions, and dealing with the multitude of emotions that I would experience as a result, was to make a call to their father. I made the call and the only question I asked was "why did you call Shae, instead of me, with the news of Tyrell?" The call was short because he became angry, would not answer the question and simply hung up. He then called Shae and told her that I did not want him to help with packing up Tyrell's belongings; that he would not go.

When I heard this accounting of the conversation from Shae, I exploded in a fury that I had not felt for a very, very long time. For 23 years I had endured their father demeaning me to the children. It was years after they left home before they learned who I really was; rather than the person that their father depicted me to be. As I had always spoken positively to the children, of their father, it was as if I had reached critical mass and simply burst. I decided that Shae and Caleb were adults, and that I no longer had to refrain from speaking my truth.

While this was quite liberating, we were all suffering from a tremendous loss and my new found freedom to express myself on this topic did nothing to support my children, or ease their pain. It was a grievous period, and a contributing factor to the subsequent estrangement from my daughter. There were several months that my son and I were painfully polarized as well.

I made the assumption that because we were all so close, and that I had *been there* for my children emotionally, financially, etc., they would be there for me during this most difficult time in my life. That proved to be merely a slanted version of expectations on my part, and the results were distressing for everyone. The knowledge that my internal disconnection with my feelings, resulted in severing awareness of my actions, was utterly soul crushing.

As the months passed, Caleb and I were able to repair our relationship and I feel that we are stronger and closer. We have walked to the chasm of our souls and looked within. Through that process we secured a deeper understanding of ourselves, and one another. Through grace, and love, we have healed. I am deeply grateful for Caleb's willingness to work through the pain, for faithfully holding dear the memory of his brother, and for the precious gift that I received on 15 August 2009.

I had wanted to attend a Marine Birthday Ball with Tyrell but each year he was on deployment. Since both he and I had just returned from abroad, I did not consider going to the 2007 celebration. At the time, I was confident there would be many opportunities over the years.

As Caleb and Hope planned their wedding in Cancun, Caleb did his part in planning the mother-son dance. When he shared it with me, I wept as I listened to the beautiful song that my son had chosen. When it came time for our special dance at the reception, I was completely present. To see the joy in my son's eyes was priceless and I knew that it was a moment I would cherish forever. At the conclusion of the dance he placed Tyrell's dog tags, which he had worn during the ceremony, around my neck and kissed my cheek. It was Caleb who gave me a dance with my son; and this was what I wanted.

As painful as the discord was between my children, it was a catalyst for deep personal growth for me. It was when I acknowledged that my children were no longer *children* that I began to look at how I interacted with them. Whereas I was certainly there for them and provided love, support and guidance, I also was the initiator of the relationship. It is good, and right, that a mother anticipate the needs of her child. However, as the child matures, it is necessary for the mother to step back and allow the child to expand and explore their own identity.

I always told my children that the day a child can look their parent in the eye, and state who they are without fear, is the day that the child begins an adult-to-adult relationship with their parent. Although I was confident that I did not impose my beliefs or expectations on my children, I realized that I had not given them the appropriate space in order for them to develop their own sense of identity. I realized that I was not the great and wonderful mother that I *thought* I was.

I was actually shocked to make this discovery. In essence it shattered the illusions that I had created about myself, about my relationship with my children, and how I defined myself as a mother. I had considered my relationship with my daughter and my sons to be exceptional. My daughter and I were also close friends who shared many journeys together. My relationship with my sons was blessed with an openness that I always treasured. Whereas I had thought the relationship with my children to be extremely close and reciprocal, I became aware that I had never allowed them to choose what type of relationship they wanted with me.

As I began to explore the implications of my discovery, I experienced a whole new level of grief and loss. My role of mother was the one thing that I believed I had done well. Once the delusion was destroyed, I was left with an emptiness that took considerable time to accept and integrate into my being. I had lost my oldest son, and I had again lost my family as well. As I acknowledged the reality, I became focused on how I would recreate my identity as a mother. I realized that it was necessary to release my children in a way that I had not previously considered.

I had a discussion with my son, and wrote a letter to my daughter, where I expressed my regret and sorrow for not recognizing this earlier and explained that they now had the opportunity to decide what type of relationship they wanted to have with me. They had the freedom to meet *their* needs instead of succumbing to me and my version of auto-pilot motherhood.

While this self-discovery was indeed excruciating, the ability to acknowledge it and move through it created healing. It was a journey that taught me the immense power of love and forgiveness; for myself, and for others. When we come from this place, all things become possible; and we manifest light to guide ourselves and those who journey with us.

DAYTON WILLIAMS

Be who you are and say what you feel, because those who mind don't matter, and those who matter don't mind.

—Dr. Seuss

spirituality

One thing is certain. A tragedy will bring one to their knees and expose their core belief system; not only of themselves, but of everything else. It was fitting that I was the last to see my son's body, that I was the one who placed his ashes in the niche, and that I was the one who scattered his remaining ashes by a stream. I carried my son in my womb for nine months and nurtured him for his 31 years on this earth. This was natural, for I am the mother.

During the first several weeks after Tyrell's death, I slept very little. Each evening, as I laid my head upon my pillow and closed my eyes, I saw him lying in the road: alone and suffering. The image would wrench my stomach into piercing spasms and I would begin to sob uncontrollably. I could not bear to think what his last moments on this earth were like. I could not bear to acknowledge that I was not there for him; that I did not wake when he passed. How could I not know? I had always been so connected to my children. I often experienced a *sixth sense* with them and was there for them throughout their life. I was horrified that I had failed Tyrell. And each night, I went through the same thoughts, the same feelings and restful sleep eluded me.

It was during this time that I began to ask spirit to release me from this earth. In truth, I would beg. And each morning I would awaken and realized that I was still breathing; that I would have to make it through another day. Although there was certainly a component of depression, it was more that I was merely weary to the core. I *believed* that moving through the grief would take more energy, and more courage, than I had within me. The immense degree of rawness that exposed every cell of my body exploded in agony with every tear that was shed. Often I did not even recognize myself. Gone were acceptance, tolerance, strength and balance: the very qualities that defined who I was. It was more than I could endure.

I have lived a challenging life and overcome many, many obstacles. I spent the previous 25 years on a path of healing that took me on magnificent journeys and through deep introspections. I had secured two degrees and a successful career. I had done just about everything that I wanted to do short of seeing the Northern Lights, and traveling to New Zealand. I had experienced a wonderful relationship with my children and had magnificent friends in my life. I could easily leave this earth fully satisfied, and grateful for my time here. We leave this earth when we have accomplished what we came here to do. Although this is one of my core beliefs, it did not preclude me from asking for release.

A journey is a series of steps that transverse a period of time. During the course of the journey, one will encounter great sadness, tremendous joy, numerous obstacles, deep compassion and extensive love. This is the nature of a journey for it represents the range of emotions and experiences that are a part of the human condition.

The journey takes us where we need to go and affords us encounters with others who offer their assistance. There will be times that we, and others, are not awake to the experiences. Nevertheless, the journey offers us the opportunity to explore our inner self and expand through the process. The journey is always a journey of the soul. And the experiences are tailored in such a way that they compel us to a greater truth and awareness of ourselves.

Wherever I have traveled, wherever my journey has taken me, the one constant is my relationship with spirit. God, higher power, creator, universe, there are many names however they all describe the omniscient presence that is beyond our physical sight. It is this presence that sustained me. Most of the time on this journey I have been alone or by myself. At the times when it appeared that even the light in my soul was extinguished, and my heart shattered beyond repair, I could feel the presence of spirit. Even through the rivers of tears, I could feel love surrounding me, nurturing me, supporting me. I could acknowledge, even at times faintly, that I was being cared for. Without this, I would have lost all hope. Without this, I could not have continued to get out of bed and put one foot in front of the other.

As the months passed, I would continue to ask for release from this earth. However, the intervals would be longer and I began to accept that I would continue to walk through the grief process. When I did not think that I could continue on, I found that I could learn how to be gentle with myself. I could accept grace and open myself to the gifts that would come to me in my hour of need.

It was less than 90 days after Tyrell's death and I was talking with my daughter on the phone. It happened to be one of my darkest periods. The blackness had so enclosed me; so consumed me; that I struggled to stay engaged with life. I had lost my way and could not find a path in the darkness. Once we concluded the call, I went to bed and wept until exhaustion overcame me and I fell asleep.

The next morning, a little before 8:00a, there was a knock on my door. It was my daughter. She had been up most of the night and left Dallas around 4:30a. She held a rope and a flashlight and told me that she would help me find my way through the darkness. At that moment, grace touched my heart and I released a flood of despair through my tears. I was deeply moved by the love and sacrifice that she extended to me.

My alcoholism, which nearly took my life, proved to be one of my greatest gifts. It was the experience that taught me the true meaning of grace and took me on a journey that has spanned more than two and a half decades of personal growth, and developing a deep relationship with spirit. It was this experience that often provided the courage to embrace the deepest loss that I had ever known.

There are, in fact, several similarities between my journey to sobriety and my journey to living without my son. In each it was a process that took time. It was not something that I could rush through or intellectualize about. I could not, through sheer will power, change how I felt. I had to take the steps that resulted in thousands of steps that spanned a significant period of time. It was important to be open to the experiences, as well as the changes, for there was a multitude of each.

Before Tyrell's death, I could define my belief system easily. I believed that there are only two places that one can come from: fear or love. I believed that each of us are on a journey and that whatever happens is part of our personal journey, and this includes the point that we leave this earth. I believed that everything happened for a reason, and that there are no coincidences. I believed that thoughts create. I believed that children are a gift and that mine were entrusted to me to raise them to become independent adults that contribute to our society. I believed that the most important thing that I had accomplished was being a mother.

It wasn't that Tyrell's death changed my beliefs. Rather his death challenged my beliefs and offered me the opportunity to confirm that my beliefs were sound and that they were, in truth, my beliefs. His death also enabled me to see from another perspective. Just because I have a belief does not supersede that I will not experience deep emotions as a result of an event. More importantly, I learned the extent of my humanity and the depth of my spiritual foundation. It is a true statement: it is not what happens in our lives that matters; it is how we respond to what happens that matters.

Life is continuously reframing the questions: Who are you? What do you believe? How will you respond? The reframing occurs as a result of the events in our lives. At each event, we have the opportunity to reaffirm who we are, or to respond in a manner that is against our true nature, which is love. This is the choice that each of us has every minute of every day.

Nothing worth doing is completed in our lifetime:
Therefore, we are saved by hope.
Nothing true or beautiful or good makes complete sense in
Any immediate context of history:
Therefore, we are saved by faith.
Nothing we do, however virtuous, can be accomplished alone:
Therefore, we are saved by love.
No virtuous act is quite as virtuous from the standpoint of our friend or
foe as from our own:
Therefore, we are saved by the final form of love, which is forgiveness.
—Reinhold Niebuhr

celebrating

To celebrate is a way to honor; whether it is an event or a life. This is why celebrating was so important to me and why I found numerous ways, over an extended period of time, to celebrate. The first celebration was publically held on the Sunday before we positioned Tyrell's ashes in their final resting place. There would follow countless celebrations: some public, some private and some that would not appear to be a celebration to anyone but me.

I used the first year to my advantage as there were a multitude of *firsts* where Tyrell was no longer with us. The first holidays, his first birthday; the list is extensive. There were three events that were especially important to me and offered a wealth of opportunity to celebrate: the first birthday that Tyrell was no longer with us;

the scattering of his ashes; and the planting of the tree with the scattering of his remaining ashes.

To laugh often and much, to win the respect of intelligent people and the affection of children, to earn the appreciation of honest critics and endure the betrayal of false friends, to appreciate beauty, to find the best in others, to leave the world a bit better, whether by a healthy child, a garden patch . . . . to know even one life has breathed easier because you have lived. This is to have succeeded!
—*Ralph Waldo Emerson*

the first birthday that tyrell was no longer with us

Since Tyrell was born on Christmas Day, I consumed the entire month of December in finding ways to celebrate. I chose opportunities that would either honor Tyrell, or represent something that I could do on his behalf; something that he would do if he was still with us.

I donated money to the USO to support the men and women who would be separated from their families during the holiday season. My donation to the Marines Helping Marines was especially important as I have tremendous respect for all the work that they are accomplishing in their Wounded Warriors program. I visited one of Tyrell's close friends and took the boys, with the help of their mom, shopping for toys. I sent the money that I would have given Tyrell for his birthday to a man, and his family.

As strange as it may seem, I had to buy something for Tyrell. Not to do so, was too painful to contemplate. This young man was important to Tyrell, and to me, and he became a surrogate son who helped me get through a very difficult time; my son's first birthday after his death. Words fall short in expressing my gratitude.

I was blessed with several offers to spend Christmas with friends and I struggled with a decision as to what to do. It would have been wonderful to be with my friends; to receive their hugs of support and see their eyes filled with love. I was particularly struggling with Sonja's invitation because I had not seen her since our going away party, and we had spoken on several occasions regarding me making a trip to Florida. In the end, though, I knew that I needed to be alone. This was the first birthday, and it would never come again. How I spent this day would be a foundation from which I would build on, and it would support me in future birthdays.

I learned from Sheri of the Yahrzeit Light and picked one up at the grocery store. I also stopped by the bakery and ordered a cake. My next stop was the aisle where the balloons and candles were located. I picked up a couple of packages of red balloons and a box of candles. I left the grocery store and stopped at the liquor store, the cigar store and Best Buy: whiskey, cigars and Mama Mia DVD. On Christmas Eve I picked up the cake and lit the Yahrzeit. My celebration had begun.

I awoke Christmas morning with all of the anticipation of a child. I was grateful that my heart was light and that I could spend the day doing whatever came to me. The first thing I did was check on the Yahrzeit, and was pleased to see that is still burned bright. Next I removed the cake from the refrigerator and placed it on the counter. After I counted out 32 candles, I tenderly placed them around the cake. Since I would later share the balloons with Sadie, I blew up about a dozen before I ran out of oxygen.

I then went to my room to get *birthday bear*. Birthday bear was given to me about 20 years prior by one of my dear friends, Cindy. Each year I pulled birthday bear off the shelf and sang happy birthday to myself while he provided the music. I brought birthday bear into the breakfast room and Sadie became ecstatic. She was certain that the balloons, and the bear, were for her. She eventually got the balloons, which most likely helped her forget all about the bear.

With Sadie at my side, I lit the candles and birthday bear and I sang Happy Birthday over and over. I laughed; I cried; and I sang until the need passed. With a blessing on my lips, and tears flowing down my cheeks, I blew out the candles.

Sadie and I spent about 30 minutes playing with the balloons. This was a game that the boys had created. They would bat a balloon between them while Sadie raced back and forth, whining, and barking and all the while lunging for the balloon. It was a game that brought intense delight to everyone and laughter always filled the air when the *game was on.* Sadie had a distinct advantage since it was just she and I. As soon as she would catch and pop the balloon, she would look at me with anticipation for the next balloon. We managed to get through half of the balloons before we both tired.

Feeling uplifted, I decided it was time to watch Mama Mia. I was very much looking forward to the movie as it was a connection to Sweden; even the package made me smile as I pulled the DVD from the box. The next 100 minutes were filled with delight beyond measure. Once the movie concluded, I restarted it and activated the on-screen lyrics so I could sing along. I sang. I danced. I laughed. I cried. It was a joyous time and a wonderful way to celebrate this special day. As the credits rolled across the screen, I decided it was now time to eat cake.

After I finished my cake, I retreated to the porch to smoke my cigar. Smoking the cigar was akin to riding the Harley to Austin for the spreading of Tyrell's ashes. Both were things that Tyrell loved and I did them on his behalf. As I sat in my chair, I began to speak from my heart to Tyrell. I expressed thoughts and feelings that reflected my journey of the previous ten months.

I talked about how I wished things were different and how much I missed his laughter and his sparkling eyes. I talked about how much I missed *him*, and how much I missed my family. I talked about all the changes that I had experienced and how they left me feeling disjointed and disconnected from myself. I talked about my love for him and gratitude for this constant in my life. I sent him my blessing and celebrated the peace and freedom of the space that he now occupied. As tears ran down my cheeks, I imagined him soaring on the wings of the eagles.

Shortly after I finished my cigar, Caleb and Hope stopped by and I was elated to see them. I asked if they would join me in a toast to Tyrell, and I poured whiskey for them and a cola for me. With Sadie beside us, we took turns with a toast and drank to Tyrell. It was a glorious day, and as I placed my head upon my pillow later that evening, I gave thanks for the love that was bursting from my heart. I had taken another step toward healing.

scattering the ashes

I had imagined that I would ride on the back of a Harley and scatter Tyrell's ashes across the University of Texas campus. This thought came to me because it was where Tyrell wanted to secure his degree. Whereas Shae, Caleb and I are all Aggies, Tyrell wanted to be a Longhorn. The thought continues to shape a smile on my face, as it was typical of Tyrell to move to the rhythm of his own drum.

There were many times that I thought of scattering the ashes, however, for various reasons it would never come to fruition. I never expected that more than a year would pass before I completed the task. As it turns out, and is often the case, it was merely the *right* time.

Near the end of March 2009, Tom stopped by one evening to visit with Caleb. I mentioned that I wanted to scatter Tyrell's ashes and explained that I needed to make the trip to Austin on a Harley. Tom graciously offered to assist. No further plans were made except we would leave on the morning of 5 April around 9:00a. What transpired is another example of a god deal. It was a perfect day, in a perfect place, with the perfect group of people. We totaled 11 and I was moved by the number as Tyrell passed on the 11th.

We left Bryan with a caravan: Tom and I on his Harley, Caleb and Hope in his '64 Chevy and Lopez and Courtné brought up the rear. We made two stops along the way. The first, I learned, was where Tom and Tyrell had stopped when they were on a road trip. It was the first trip that Tyrell had made on his bike. The second stop was to hook up with Mike. Once we reached Austin, we met up with Tommy and Erin, and Trent and Adrian at the University of Texas.

An unanticipated circumstance arose. UT was having an event on campus. The campus was swarming with people and the plan of riding through campus, while releasing a small container of ashes, began to sound like a *really bad idea.* I am certain that the City of Austin, and all of the folks on campus, would have agreed wholeheartedly. It now became Tommy's responsibility to locate a suitable place for the scattering. Caleb handed me the container, which held the ashes, and I placed it in my jacket. We pulled away from the curb and our amplified caravan went into motion traveling through the streets of Austin.

My gaze remained on Tommy's truck and I noticed that he had pulled into a parking lot which serviced a park just north of campus. As I walked around I discovered a trail that began a short distance from where I stood. I walked towards the trail and was greeted by a dragonfly. I was quite excited for a dragonfly is known to represent renewal after a great hardship.

As I followed my newly revealed guide down the path, it took a curve and I noticed a landmark. I began laughing with sheer delight. I was welcomed by the trunk of a tree that was, most likely, struck by lightning as there were no branches. Upon the trunk a face was painted in blue. The face seemed to explode with mischievous laughter and I could imagine Tyrell saying *"isn't this great!"* I raced back to get Caleb and he, too, grinned when he saw the landmark.

Caleb and I returned to retrieve our friends. As we strolled down the trail, and upon passing the landmark, we were greeted by the most magnificent scene. A glade arose before us with a running brook outlining the east side. It was a beautiful place, and as the sun filtered through the trees my eyes began to moist. I was profoundly touched by the gloriousness that surrounded me.

I asked that we take a moment to say our farewells to Tyrell. Let it be a personal moment so that we could fully express that which was in our hearts. I stepped away from the group, and towards the brook, to release the ashes of my son. A few ashes escaped, and as I witnessed their flight, I knew the wind would take them through the city that Tyrell cherished. I expressed my love, sent my blessings, and briefly paused to simply savor the moment. As the words *thank you* escaped my lips, I returned to the group and announced that it was time to eat and have a beer in Tyrell's honor.

We gathered at the Mellow Mushroom for food, drink and laughter. As I sat looking around at everyone, I was stirred by the understanding that each was present because they wanted to be. Even after all this time they gathered to honor Tyrell. This moved me deeply and I was grateful to celebrate this wondrous event with this special group of friends.

While Tom offered me a ride back to Bryan, I graciously declined. The ride up had been harrowing. The wind was relentless and there were several times that I thought I would have the opportunity to *literally* fly; if only for a brief time. I was also experiencing a weird gait that I knew would stay with me for a few days. Although I thought that I had adequate padding on my backside, I never considered how much was required for a 2.5 hour ride. I had fulfilled my goal and made the trip to Austin on a Harley; and assured myself that this was *good enough*. Laying in the backseat of a car, warm and cozy and away from the bone chilling wind, sounded like heaven at this point.

Once we arrived home, we viewed all of the pictures that Hope had taken. I discovered tears of joy gently flowing down my cheeks. Hope had eloquently captured the day and our purpose. Once again I had the opportunity to express my gratitude for I had asked Hope if she would be willing to take the pictures, and she had graciously accepted. It was truly a glorious day.

scattering the ashes around the tree

The only ashes that remained were in a small urn, called a keepsake urn. I pondered what to do with these ashes for a long time. Originally I had given them away however I strongly felt that it was necessary to release them to the earth, and to the wind, and requested they be returned to me.

I wanted to plant a tree at the house, in honor of Tyrell, and I wanted Caleb to have input as to the type of tree. He conversed with Hope and the requirements were simple; it needed to be a climbing tree. I contacted a local arborator and discussed my needs regarding a tree to plant. He came back with several suggestions and we settled on a Chinese Pistache.

My only request was to ensure that it was one which the leaves would turn red in the fall. In actuality, we had missed the optimum planting period which is in November; we were planting in April. The arborator explained that it was necessary to water the tree weekly and that if it made it through the summer, most likely all would be well.

On the afternoon of 3 May 2009, Caleb, Hope, Sadie and I stood around the tree representing north, south, east and west. Caleb and Hope were much more amenable to my requests than Sadie, who represented south radically different than the other directions. Caleb worked hard to secure her cooperation and it suddenly occurred to me that Tyrell was bursting with laughter as he watched over us.

We decided to let Sadie be Sadie, and began to move clockwise around the circle starting with Hope. Each said a few words and scattered some ashes around the tree. I concluded by reading my short message and scattered the remaining ashes. We completed our ceremony with a celebration at Abuelo's, which was one of Tyrell's favorite restaurants. As we drove to the restaurant, it occurred to me that it was the last restaurant Tyrell, Caleb and I went to. It was the perfect way to end a magnificent celebration.

Each day I would walk to the backyard and spend time with the tree. I did this every day until one day I noticed that all of the ashes were gone. At first I was sickened and felt as if I had been viciously punched in the stomach. After the feeling passed, and I regained my ability to breathe, I spent some time reflecting. Prior to this moment, the focus had been on the ashes instead of on my original purpose for planting the tree; a memorial to my son. Now that the ashes were gone, I could once again focus on the tree and how it would forever remain a beautiful reminder of Tyrell.

As I closed my eyes, I could almost hear into the future. The air sparkled with the laughter of my grandchildren while they played beneath the tree.

closure

As with grief, closure is a process. I often suspected that they ran parallel paths, and as I moved through one I moved through the other. The process was both exacerbated and supported by the fact that the person who struck and killed my son was never identified. During the aftermath, when I began to deduce there was the strong probability that the police would never identify the person, I imagined what would happen if it were otherwise.

First the police would apprehend the person and they would be placed in jail. Perhaps they would be released on bail as they waited for their trial. The trial would begin, many months later, and the event would be relived as I would sit across the courtroom and listen to the testimonies. The person would take the stand and their attorney would craft a defense of extenuating circumstances. The jury of their peers would convey a sentence of 10 years and the person would be released 4 years and 3 months later.

When I began to explore this scenario, I grasped the enormity of the possibilities. No amount of time served would bring back my son. No amount of time served would equal what I had lost. In many ways, providing a short sentence would be worse; it would be as if the jury was saying that the life of my son was insignificant.

Had the person been identified, my journey of healing would have taken a completely different path; there would have been the opportunity to focus my feelings on the person, and what they *did.* There is a vast difference in focusing on another person as the cause of my grief, as opposed to focusing on the fact that Tyrell left this earth because it was his time. The person, whom I refer to as the phantom, merely assisted Tyrell in his passing. It would have been no different if he had died in Iraq; w*ho* caused his death would most likely never have been known.

This reflection, however, did not prevent me from calling the detective periodically and seek an update. I could not fathom how my son could be hit by a truck, and lie in the street directly across from the sports bar for 45 minutes, without anyone seeing anything. I could not imagine striking a person down and leaving the scene; leaving them to die. If Tyrell had been struck in Iraq, his Marine brothers would have done everything within their power to help him. They would not have left him to die alone. It was not until he was hit for the second time, and nearly a third, that a call was made to the police.

I have often thought of the woman who struck him the second time. How she must have suffered thinking that she had killed someone. How she must have agonized as she waited for the emergency vehicles to be dispatched and questioned by the authorities. Without a doubt she experienced her own horrendous trauma and it is my hope that she, too, has recovered.

The last time I spoke with the detective I requested to be put in contact with Crime Stoppers. I wanted to provide my own funds to support identifying the person and bringing them to justice. I never heard back from anyone. I left a voice mail on the last three calls that I made to the detective and never received a call back. In truth, the fact that no one was identified in the early weeks speaks volumes. As more time passes, the likelihood of closing the case diminishes exponentially.

At times I made calls to the detective because I did not know what else to do. The mother in me *needed* to do something; *needed* to do this on behalf of my son. Because the person was never identified, it supported me in focusing my energies on healing. This could be viewed as a blessing in disguise and is often how I chose to see it.

As I accepted the phantom would remain forever the phantom, I wanted something that was concrete which I could identify as movement past the tragedy; something that would give birth to light and splendor from the ugliness and sorrow. Becoming the donor of a service or hearing dog for a veteran became the medium. I contacted Sheri, President of Texas and Hearing Service Dogs, and asked her how much it would cost to support a Team; the training of a recipient and their dog. She responded with the amount of

$17,000. She told me that if I raised $10,000 she would consider it my military discount. While I was extremely grateful for the discount, $10,000 remained a daunting number.

It was the receipt of the letter from President Bush that gave me hope of attaining my dream. If I could send an email to the president and receive a response, then the possibility of raising the funds appeared attainable. While the thought was completely illogical, it somehow made absolute sense within my soul. By September 2008 the funds had been secured through the generosity of friends and family.

It would be another 11 months before a recipient was identified and many more months before I would be able to remove my son's dog tags. The wearing of the dog tags was another aspect of my closure process. I vowed to wear them until a recipient, and their dog, had been identified. The tag on the smaller chain would be transferred to the dog, and the tag on the larger chain would be placed wherever I decided would give me the most joy.

It never occurred to me that the process of locating a recipient would take more than a year. During the first year I spent an enormous amount of time sending letters and visiting with people attempting to secure their support in locating a recipient. I met, or spoke, with countless individuals that offered compassion and many took steps to do what they could to help. Nevertheless, nothing materialized.

At times it was distressing to witness all of my efforts produce absolutely nothing. I would become restless and disheartened.

I would feel that I could not bear to wear the dog tags another day and reconsider my vow. These feelings would ebb and flow and I would revisit, again and again, the concept of trust and patience. The memorial for my son would manifest at the appropriate time.

> *In the final analysis, the questions of why bad things happen to good people transmutes itself into some very different questions, no longer asking why something happened, but asking how we will respond, what we intend to do now that it happened.*
> *—Harold S. Kushner, Rabbi*

epilogue

My journey has not always been easy, however, it has not always been difficult either. The first sentence, in one of my favorite books, M. Scott Peck's *The Road Less Traveled,* is "Life is difficult." When I read that sentence for the first time, there was a resounding *yes* flooding my conscience. Today I understand the true essence of the sentence. Some days are full of joy and delightful experiences; some days begin with a blackness descending on my soul that is so heavy, and so absolute, that the very act of breathing is painful.

And then there are the other days. They are a mixture of joys and sorrows, laughter and tears, the extraordinary and the mundane. This is life, and it is life for all of us. Our ability to experience a vast array of emotions is what defines us as human. And ultimately they are what quantify our existence on this earth.

I often wonder why I am here; why I continue to wake every morning. In essence my question is "what is my purpose?" I know that I must have a reason for *being*. Some have said that our purpose is to live every day to the fullest extent. And while I agree that is a good definition, it does not answer the question as to what is *my* purpose. I believe that I must have a purpose. There must be a contribution that is unique to me; something that only I can provide.

For some their purpose is so profound that they begin to fulfill it at a very early age: the composer, the artist, the athlete. We hear these remarkable stories and are in awe. However, I do not think that purpose necessarily equates to greatness. Rather it equates to blissfulness. Those that have found their bliss have found their purpose.

And for many, our purpose changes and evolves as we change and evolve. Since change is the most constant presence in our lives, we may continuously be challenged to recreate our bliss, to redefine our purpose. For those who have had a traumatic and life altering experience this is especially true.

When I explored the option of nursing, and made the decision to move the Galveston, I thought that I had identified my purpose. I was both relieved and anxious to begin this next chapter of my life. I arrived in Galveston and began to establish a routine around work and school and explored volunteer opportunities that would allow me to be of service to others. I thought that I was in the perfect place for renewal. Galveston was a community that had experienced a tremendous tragedy in September 2008 with the devastation of

Hurricane Ike. Perhaps I could learn from the inhabitations who exhibited such courage in rebuilding their lives. Perhaps we could help one another.

Around the third week of October I began to listen to the gnawing disquiet that was building within. Something did not seem quite *right* regarding my pursuit of nursing. I logged onto the UTMB website and began to review all the programs offered in the Health Sciences. As I read details of the Occupational Therapy program, I grew more and more invigorated because it was as if the information was written just for me. As I researched the profession, I realized that this was exactly what I had been searching for. I submitted a request for additional information and waited for a response.

In reviewing the pre-requisites I was relieved to find that the Anatomy & Physiology class that I was currently taking was also required for OT. I had two courses that had been approved for the nursing program which would require verification of acceptability for OT as well. When I received a response the next day, I replied with my questions regarding the courses. I was not concerned when I did not receive a reply that week as I would be attending the Open House on Saturday; the literature indicated that we would have the opportunity to review previous courses at the Open House.

During the Open House we were encouraged to get our applications in early if we were applying for Fall 2010. While I had not established when I would submit my application, as I awoke the following morning I was clear. I spent the entire day completing all the forms and requesting transcripts from previous universities. The following week I began to apply to the universities that I would need to attend in Spring 2010 in order to meet all requirements; it would require that I attend three different colleges in order to make this work.

I also had to complete 20 hours of volunteer work, in the OT field, and this was where I was extremely fortunate to meet Karen. Karen helped me complete my volunteer requirements, and offered me multiple venues to explore. Her warmth, and passion for her profession, was contagious and I was deeply inspired by her commitment to her work.

The first three weeks in November were filled will numerous activities in securing acceptance to the universities so that I could enroll in classes. As open registration began 13 November and 18 November, and I had specific classes I need to take, I was beginning to feel a little stress. By the time I received approval from the first university to register, the class had filled. I sent an email to the professor requesting to be forced into the course. He responded with his approval within an hour. One down: one to go.

Once I received acceptance into the second university, one of the courses had already filled. Concurrently, I had contacted the professor who led the Open House and requested information regarding the first round of interviews. I learned that the interviewees had already been identified. My completed application had not been received in time; therefore, I was not even in the running. I mentioned the outstanding review of my courses and she asked that I send them to her and she would review them and get back to me later in the afternoon.

When I read her response I was disheartened. Neither class would suffice which meant that I would be required to take 19 hours in the spring semester. This was simply not feasible; even if I quit my job. I phoned her and thanked her for the response and asked if the admissions committee would allow me to take the two courses in the summer. She said that she would submit the request and asked that I send a mail with the supporting details.

I had hoped that I would be in the first round of interviews and I would know, before the end of the year, if I had been accepted into the program. As it now stood, the next round of interviews would not occur until February or March; long after spring semester begins. If I secured approval to take summer classes, and I had not yet received a response, I still had the hurdle of getting forced into one of the classes in the spring.

There comes a point when I simply stop; and I had reached that place in pursuing admittance into the OT program. Over the years I have learned that often things are not as they appear. Consequently, the best I can do is to be clear on what I want, listen to my inner guide, and then do my part.

I cannot explain why I was inspired to pursue OT, received such a favorable response, and then everything came to a screeching halt. It may have been solely to feel inspired once again. It may have been to experience the OT field and meet some wonderful people in the process. Whatever the reason, I know that there was *a* reason and that the experience was valuable.

I will take some time to regroup and then return to action. Until I determine my direction, I will most likely only take Anatomy and Physiology II in the spring. This keeps me on target for nursing if that proves to be my path. More importantly it keeps me moving forward.

What happens next is not known; nor have I reached the end of my journey. I still have Tyrell's phone number listed in my mobile; and I still have his email in my contact list. Moving forward in certain areas has taken noticeably longer than others. When I glance over the previous months, and recognize the 2nd year anniversary is approaching, I acknowledge that I have made considerable progress. The *gentlest* thing to do is accept the positive; and trust that the remainder will happen at the appropriate time, and in due time.

I attempt to imagine what it would be like to be a child again. For a healthy child is full of wonder, has countless dreams, and a world of infinite possibilities. I visualize this as I hope to learn from the child. What do I want to do? What do I want to manifest in my life? How do I want to contribute? Depending on one's perspective, this place of unlimited potentials can invoke excitement or dread. My intent is to embrace this opportunity with enthusiasm; and learn to release myself to the possibilities. Not only is this healthy, it is a far better alternative.

Whatever path I take, I will continue to heal. I will continue to experience ways to recapture my passion for life. I will continue to be open so that my heart will smile again. This I choose: in honor of my son; in honor of myself.

Live with intention.
Walk to the edge.
Listen hard.
Practice wellness.
Play with abandon.
Laugh.
Choose with no regret.
Continue to learn.
Appreciate your friends.
Do what you love.
Live as if this is all there is.
—Mary Anne Radmacher

picture gallery

I hitched a ride with Tom for the spreading of Tyrell's ashes.

Tyrell is standing on top of the vehicle. 2nd Tour in Iraq.

Caleb standing next to the landmark.

My father created this sign for Tyrell's welcome home celebration from his 2nd tour. Everyone is absolutely beaming with delight.

Shae riding her Harley. Tyrell would be proud.

We gathered at the Mellow Mushroom after the scattering
of Tyrell's ashes. These are dear friends of both my sons and
they have supported all of us every step of the way.

Tyrell and his faithful companion Sadie.

Tyrell and I dressed up for Sonya's and my going away party
in Boulder. The Sports Bar didn't know what hit them.

Caleb and Hope's wedding day in Cancun. It was a glorious celebration.

This became the last capture of our joy and laughter together as a family: Shae, Tyrell, me, and Caleb. The picture is especially precious as Tyrell is holding a *Welcome Home* sign from his 3rd tour. My dear young friend, Viktoria, created the sign which I brought from Sweden.

letter to president bush

While sending mails to my team thanking them for their contribution on a particular project is something that I consistently do, I also send *thank you* mails when I am having a particularly challenging day and feeling that I am not making any sort of progress. I find the exercise of expressing gratitude therapeutic. It performs a shift in my psyche and I secure another viewpoint that is positive and uplifting.

On 22 February 2008, three days before I buried my son, I sat at my computer to write a *thank you* email to President Bush. As the days passed, I would consistently look in my inbox for a response. One day I mentioned to the children that I had not yet received a response from the president. I detected the look that I often saw on their faces when they were not quite sure what to say. "You think that you are going to receive a response?" "Of course", I replied. What I envisioned was a general response with condolences. Nothing out of the ordinary, but I felt that I would receive a response.

What I did not anticipate was receiving an overnight package on a Saturday morning. Enclosed was a beautiful letter on gold-embossed stationary, and a brass medallion with the president's name on one side and Commander in Chief on the other. Tears of gratitude filled my eyes, and I was deeply touched by the gifts that I held in my hands. I sent a blessing to the president, and his family, and to those that made this possible.

22 february 2008

Dear President Bush,

On behalf of my son, Tyrell Seth Williams, I am writing this letter to you. As a result of Tyrell hearing one of your speeches regarding terrorism, he signed up to serve in the United States Marine Corps in 2003. During his 4.5 years of service, he completed 3 tours in Iraq. He was not obligated to serve the third tour, however, he wanted to support his brothers and do his part to ensure they stayed safe.

Tyrell was honorably discharged, at the rank of Sergeant, in November 2007, and returned to Bryan, TX. On 20 December, 5 days before his 31st birthday, he moved to Austin, TX to begin his new life. During the next 6 weeks, Tyrell was the happiest that I have ever seen him. He was passionate about living in Austin and explored the city in depth. He was in the process of enrolling in college, and applying for jobs. He was purchasing household items and establishing a comfortable life. In sports terms, 'he was at the top of his game'.

Everything ended when, on 11 February 2008, he was struck by a hit-and-run driver and fatally injured. At this time, we still have no information or leads as to who was responsible for this tragedy. While we deeply mourn the loss of a man that was a son, grand-son, brother, friend and Marine, we take comfort in the fact that Tyrell served his country with honor, returned safely to us, and that we were all able to spend several joyful weeks together. We had the opportunity to witness the amazing changes that had occurred, as a direct result, of his service in the United States Marine Corps. Tyrell entered the Corps searching for meaning and direction to his life. He exited the Corps a strong man who knew that he had a purpose, and he was honored to have served his country and support his brothers.

As the Commander—in-Chief, I want you know what a powerful effect that you had on Tyrell. He was deeply moved by your speech, and this radically changed his life forever, and for the better. And, for this, I am deeply grateful. I am including below the memorial folder so that you may know how we honored our son. I considered sending the newspaper clippings of the tragic accident however this is not where I choose to direct my focus. While it is my desire that the person who took my son's life be identified and brought to justice, I also know that everything in this life happens for a reason.

I wish you the best, Mr. President. It was your influence . . . your words . . . that touched my son's heart and soul, and ultimately allowed him to serve in what he believed to be the greatest branch of our services, the United States Marine Corps. I am both honored and grateful.

Semper Fidelis,

Dayton Williams

MEMORIAL

Tyrell "Ty" Williams, 31, of Austin, TX was called home on Monday, February 11, 2008. He was born December 25, 1976 in Oklahoma City, OK. He graduated high school in Edmond, OK in 1995. He worked in various trades, and lived in a number of cities, before deciding that he wanted to serve his country and entered the U.S. Marine Corps in 2003. His 4.5 years of service included three tours of duty in Iraq, with an honorable discharge at the rank of Sergeant in November 2007. His positive outlook on life and strong spirit will be deeply missed by his surviving family, mother Dayton Williams, father Russ Williams, grand-father Ed Davis, sister Shae Williams, brother Caleb Williams, his faithful dog Sadie, and his scores of friends. The first farewell will be held in Austin, the city he chose to begin his life, at Weed-Corley-Fish on February 16, 3-5p. His ceremony will be held on February 25 at the Dallas-Fort Worth National Cemetery 11a, and we will have a celebration of his life on 24 February in Dallas. In lieu of flowers, please honor his passing by making a donation, in his name, to Texas Hearing & Service Dogs, 4803 Rutherglen, Austin, TX 78749. He made this world a more beautiful place.

Saturday, February 16, 2008
3pm-5pm Farewell in Austin, TX
Weed-Corely-Fish Funeral Home

Prior to the cremation, Ty's mom, dad, sister and brother are offering a private viewing. There will be no service held at this time.

6pm-8pm Open House at Ty's Home in Austin, TX

We are opening Ty's home for one last gathering for those who would like to stop by.

Sunday, February 24, 2008
All Day Celebration of Life for Tyrell at Shae's Home

Please join us at your leisure to celebrate Ty's wonderful 31 years of life. There is no better way to honor him than to have a celebration. His personality was to look at life in a positive manner and we would like to share that with him on this day. Stop by for a few minutes or stay all day, Shae is opening her home.

Monday, February 25, 2008
11am Internment Cemetary
Dallas-Fort Worth National Cemetery

Begin arriving at 10:45am in Lane A. This simple ceremony is a military honor with taps and the color guard presentation. After the ceremony, everyone is welcome at Shae's home.

THE WHITE HOUSE

WASHINGTON

March 17, 2008

Ms. Dayton Williams
715 Eagle Pass Street
Bryan, Texas 77802

Dear Dayton:

Your heartfelt note just reached me in the Oval Office. I am deeply saddened by the loss of your son. Brave individuals like Tyrell are what make our military the greatest force for freedom in the history of the world, and I am inspired by his devotion to duty. We will always remember his service and sacrifice, and he will forever have the respect and admiration of a grateful Nation.

Laura and I will keep you and your family in our prayers. May God bless you, and may God bless America.

Sincerely,

George W. Bush

newspaper articles

T hree articles were printed regarding Tyrell. The first one was an attempt by the police department, with the support of the media, to secure information regarding the hit-and-run. Nothing ever materialized. The second article was as a result of one of my daughter's friends, Amanda, contacting the media and requesting that another article be run. Once again nothing materialized. The third article was at my request; and my attempt to secure a recipient for a Hearing or Service Dog. My goal was not achieved.

Even though the articles did not achieve their immediate objectives, I remain deeply grateful to the media for their support and help in getting the messages to the public.

pedestrian killed after being struck by car

By Joshua Sanders | Tuesday, February 12, 2008, 05:42 AM | Austin Statesman

A pedestrian believed to be in his 30s was struck by two cars and fatally injured in Northwest Austin last night, police said. His death is Austin's 4th traffic fatality this year, according to police.

The accident happened around 11 p.m., when officers responded to an automobile/pedestrian crash in the 12100 block of Waters Park Drive. The pedestrian, whose name has not been released pending positive identification and notification of his family, was pronounced deceased at the scene.

Austin Police Department spokesman Joe Munoz said it is unclear why the pedestrian was in the roadway, but he was struck by a driver sometime after 10:30 p.m. and then again shortly after 11 p.m. The second car that struck the driver, a 2002 gray Kia Spectra traveling southbound on Waters Park, stayed at the scene until police arrived, Munoz said.

Police ask that anyone with information about the accident call APD Vehicular Homicide detectives at 974-5774 or 974-5516.

iraq veteran killed in hit-and-run was starting new life in austin

Tyrell Williams, 1976-2008

By Matt Presser
AMERICAN-STATESMAN STAFF
Thursday, February 21, 2008

After three tours of duty in Iraq with the U.S. Marine Corps, Sgt. Tyrell Williams moved to Austin to start a new chapter of his life in the city to which he had always dreamed of returning.

He had moved into a house in Northwest Austin, applied to Austin Community College and set up job interviews for last week.

But on Feb. 11, he was struck and killed by two cars, Austin police said. Williams' mother said he was walking home from a sports bar. One driver remained at the scene, police said, but the other left.

Ten days later, police still are looking for information on what happened to Williams, 31, as his family copes with the loss of a man who they say was the happiest he had ever been.

"He loved Austin. That was just his happy space," said his mother, Dayton Williams, a Bryan resident who lived in Austin with him more than 10 years ago. "He was excited to start his life, (and) it was just the place where he wanted to be."

Police say one car hit Williams sometime after 10:30 p.m. and another about 11 p.m. in the 12100 block of Waters Park Road, near the intersection of MoPac Boulevard (Loop 1) and Parmer Lane. Police would not say whether the second driver has been charged or will face charges. Because it's an ongoing investigation, police wouldn't discuss other details of the case, the fourth traffic fatality of 2008.

Williams joined the Marines in 2003 and was honorably discharged in November. He wasn't obligated to return to Iraq a third time, but he wanted to care for the younger Marines, said 1st Sgt. Aaron McDonald.

"He saw some Marines that needed someone, and he knew he could help," McDonald said. "No one waved a bonus in his face or a promotion or a medal. He just searched his soul and made a decision to help out these guys."

Shae Williams, 33, said her brother was "hit hard" by Sept. 11, 2001, and felt he could make a difference.

"The most surprising thing, of course, is that he does three tours of duty in Iraq and comes back safely and then this happens," she said.

On Saturday, a group of friends and family attended a funeral service and gathered at his house to celebrate his life. A graveside ceremony is scheduled for 11 a.m. Monday at the Dallas-Fort Worth National Cemetery.

Anyone with information on the case is asked to call Austin police Detective Mark Breckenridge at 974-5516. mpresser@statesman. com; 445-3601

after son is killed, mother finds solace in helping others

By KAYLA SLIMP
Sunday, 31 August 2008
Bryan/College Station Eagle kayla.slimp@theeagle.com

Just days after a February hit-and-run killed her son, a Bryan mother found a way to memorialize the former Marine and create a little comfort in a time of tragedy.

Rather than receiving flowers from mourners, Dayton Williams asked for donations for the training of a service dog to assist a disabled veteran. This month, she reached her $10,000 goal.

Next, she hopes to meet the person who will receive the service dog.

Sense of duty

Shortly after his 1995 graduation from Edmond High School in Oklahoma, where his father still lives, Tyrell Williams moved to Bryan with his mother and his sister, Shae Williams, a 1998 graduate of Texas A&M. He worked and lived in Bryan before joining the Marines in 2003, when he was 26.

Williams enlisted after being inspired by one of President Bush's speeches against terrorism, his mother said. The young man wanted to make a difference in the world. Sgt. Williams had served three tours in Iraq with the U.S. Marine Corps when he returned to his family in Bryan in November with a new outlook on life, Dayton Williams said. He talked about going into psychology or criminology because he wanted to help people with mental problems. "[Before he enlisted], he was looking and trying to find his purpose and place in life, and he came back, and he knew his purpose and his place," she said.

Dayton Williams said her son volunteered to serve the final tour because he wanted to help younger Marines. "We all had tremendous respect for Ty for volunteering to deploy to a combat zone for a third time," one of Williams' commanding officers wrote to his family in the days after his death. "He struck me as the kind of guy that would do something like that for no other reason than for his brothers that had fought for him."

For six weeks after he left the Marines, the Williams family enjoyed spending time with their son and brother. Williams and his younger brother, Caleb, now a senior at Texas A&M, played games and laughed constantly. "The house was just filled with so much joy and laughter," Dayton Williams said.

On Dec. 20, Williams left his family's home in Bryan to move to Austin. The 31-year-old applied to Austin Community College and started setting up job interviews. Williams' mother, sister and brother visited him Dec. 30. "We went to Austin to see him and went bowling, and he was so happy," his mother said.

The fatal accident

On the night of Feb. 11, as Williams walked home from a nearby sports bar, he was struck by two cars and killed near the intersection of MoPac Boulevard (Loop 1) and Parmer Lane. The first driver, who still hasn't been identified, left the scene; the second motorist remained with Williams until emergency workers arrived.

Early the next morning, the family learned of Williams' death.

In the days that followed, his mother suggested to the family that donations be made in Williams' honor to Texas Hearing and Service Dogs of Austin. They printed the information in both the memorial folder and the obituary.

Dayton Williams said she had started supporting this organization in October, but that she chose the group for memorial contributions because her son loved helping people and loved animals, especially his pit bull, Sadie. "Sadie and Tyrell were attached," she said. Caleb Williams took care of Sadie while his brother was in Iraq and is continuing in that responsibility.

Dayton Williams talked with Sheri Soltes, president of Texas Hearing and Service Dogs, and found out that sponsoring a dog costs $17,500. Soltes offered a military discount, bringing the cost down to $10,000, but Williams saw even the reduced rate as hopelessly out of reach. Still, she said, she wanted to help the organization as much as possible.

The motivation

Eleven days after the accident, Dayton Williams e-mailed President Bush to thank him for motivating her son to enlist. In March, she received a response. "Brave individuals like Tyrell are what make our military the greatest force of freedom in the history of the world, and I am inspired by his devotion to duty," Bush wrote. "We will always remember his service and sacrifice, and he will forever have the respect and admiration of a grateful Nation."

The short note from the president inspired Dayton Williams to raise the full $10,000. Since then, sponsoring a dog in her son's honor has been her passion and mission. "If I can e-mail the president and receive a response in the mail, I can raise $10,000," she said. "Don't ask me how those two correlate, but in my mind, they did."

The donations

Williams' friends and family responded with $9,500, including $500 from Dayton Williams and a matching grant from her employer, IBM. She told her daughter and father about her expanded endeavor, and they both donated as well.

On Aug. 15, Williams decided to withdraw the remaining $500 from her son's estate. "It's very moving because one of the ways Mrs. Williams chose to process her grief was to raise the funds for a hearing or service dog in Ty's honor," Soltes said. "It's very humbling and a great honor to be able to help in her healing process."

The money will sponsor a dog in the Assistance Dogs for Military Personnel program at the agency. The program trains hearing, service and balance dogs for disabled veterans of the Iraq and Afghanistan wars. Every dog they train is rescued, and the veteran receives the dog free, which Williams describes as "so admirable and so noble." The dogs provide veterans with both service and companionship. "When I submitted the money, my only requirement was that it be a veteran from Iraq or Afghanistan," she said. "If it is a Marine, that is, at a personal level, wonderful."

The recipient

Once the group chooses a recipient, it will match a dog in its program to the veteran's needs or secure another animal.

"We've been working hard to reach out to servicemen and women to find a recipient. We want to let them know that this service is available," Soltes said. Once someone has been chosen, Dayton Williams said, she plans to go to the training facility in Dripping Springs to meet the dog and the recipient, and she hopes to choose the dog's name.

"I wear both my son's dog tags," she said. "The day I take them off will be the day I hand the short necklace to the recipient. I will wear the long necklace." Williams also said she would like to meet the recipient at their home, wherever that may be. She hopes to remain close to the person and take them into her family, but she knows that even if that doesn't work out, she was still a part of something positive. "When Tyrell came back, it was like, 'I can breathe again. My son is home. He survived three tours.' When something happens like this, you just want something to say that this is not a waste," she said. "To me, this is a living memorial to my son. He is alive in the recipient, in the dog. This is important to me. This is my passion."

journal entries

I have often reflected on my challenge, during my journey, to write in my journal. Writing is a wonderful outlet for expression and provides a vehicle for documenting thoughts and feelings at a point in time. Anyone who has practiced journaling has benefited through the introspection that it induces. Additionally, there is the added benefit of having a marker that one can review at a future date to gauge the personal changes that have transpired over a period of time.

I am aware of the benefits, and I have experienced their power. Yet this only serves to add confusion to my lack of ability to perform something that has repeatedly brought me so much value. It becomes yet another opportunity to accept; and trust that at the appropriate time I will return to that which brings me joy.

The following journal entries are presented as originally written.

It is a gift to be able to paint a particular picture or to carve a statue, and so to make a few objects beautiful; but it is far more glorious to carve and paint the very atmosphere and medium through which we look. To affect the quality of the day—that is the highest of the arts.
—Henry David Thoreau

7 april 2008

It is a Monday afternoon and I am sitting at the airport waiting to board the plane. This is the first time that I have been out-and-about since returning to work. I am on a business trip to Phoenix and I find myself restless. I am dreading this trip. I do not have the energy, or the desire, to attend a customer meeting. This is a strange feeling for me.

In the past, it was second nature to put on the business hat and conform to the role of a professional. At this time, however, I begin to question everything: the purpose, the importance and I add a pinch of 'what's the use' for good measure. This is what grief does. It places a film over the eyes which results in distorting ones perceptions of life. Everything, it seems, takes on a different look, taste or feel. Grief even *appears* to re-arrange ones beliefs and what they previously defined as what they liked or disliked.

Before I drown in the madness exploding in my mind, I open my briefcase and take out a pen and paper and begin to write a letter. As I write, I scold myself for leaving the house without Kleenex and make the 5th trip to the restroom to gather more toilet paper. Toilet paper was never created to meet the needs and expectations of eyes and noses. I reflect on this as I notice all the white pieces flecked over my pants. I return my thoughts to my son and begin to speak to him from my heart.

Dearest Tyrell,

My dear, dear son. I am writing this mail to you as a suggestion from Paula. I had to stop and get toilet paper because I already feel the tears forming. What can I possibly say to express much I love you, and how much I miss you? There are no words in our language to express the emotion in my heart and soul. I miss you; pure and simple. I miss being able to hear your voice, and receive a hug and a kiss on my cheek. I miss your laughter, and your joy. I miss doing things for you, and helping you get settled in Austin. The list is endless because I would want to experience all these things and more . . . if I had the opportunity.

But, that option is not available to me and I must find a way to move through . . . and past . . . the grief. To be in a place that I am happy . . . truly happy . . . that you are in a better place and that you are total and pure love and joy. Right now . . . this minute . . . I am very much your mom and I am feeling my own pain. Also, I am unable to move past it . . . at this moment anyway.

I am in shock really. I was prepared . . . in a sense . . . that I could lose you in Iraq. I was not prepared for this. This . . . I never expected: an accident where you were fatally injured, and the person who did this is still at large. The irony is amazing. You endured 3 tours in Iraq to be struck dead in Austin . . . your happy place!

At this time, I have feelings of hatred for Austin. Whereas Austin was once a place that I considered moving to myself, it is now a place that I never want to see again. This, of course, could change. It is just where I am today. I am angry that it was Austin that took your life . . . that snuffed out your joy and left me with the greatest pain that I have ever experienced.

I am so glad that you came to Caleb in his dreams. That meant so much to him! He misses you so much, Tyrell. He lost his brother and his best friend! My heart breaks for him. Yet, considering everything, I think he is doing OK. He has been able to continue with school and is doing well. He is going to Mexico in May and will stay with Raffino for a few days. Hopefully the experience will help him decide if he wants to Study Abroad in Mexico or Spain next Spring. You know I have cried a lot over the fact that I did not get to send you and Caleb to Mexico! I know that you were looking forward to that as well. It was written on your whiteboard. So, I have asked Caleb to have a drink and a cigar in your honor.

I hope that you are pleased with everything that we have done regarding your passing. It was all done to honor you and I did my best to go with whatever came to me. All of the decisions were for you and it was a joint effort . . . I asked everyone for their input. I did not want months to go by and someone look back and say . . . . I wish we had done 'that'. And, I do not think we will look back with any regrets: for that, I am very happy. Shae and I have reviewed what we did and we both feel good about everything. She did a beautiful job writing your obituary and that was very important to her.

8 june 2008

I awoke at 11:30p and reached for pen and paper to write . . . .

Here I lie upon my bed
Wondering . . . will I be fed?
While I wait, I feel the pain
Of love now lost, of senseless gain

Where the heart is free to roam
The soul is nourished and yet re-born
The quest is mine, this I know
To choose; to live; to love; to grow

The question I now know is true
Will I feed myself anew?
Answer, yes! my soul cries out
Now is the time; release all doubt

Here I stand
My arms stretch wide
Open to
The boundless sky

I returned to slumber and was re-awakened at 12:20a to write . . .

Stop! I say
Cease this moment
The constant wails
The endless torment

Place your staff
Against your brow
Bow your head
And prepare to call

Upon the strength
Deep in the soul
It lies there waiting
To bestow

Your heart's desire
Your dreams of flight
Towards visions of healing
Visions of light

Lift your head
You are renewed
Grace is restored
From solitude

21 june 2008

Once again, my soul speaks . . . .

I descended to a place
Where darkness charred
My soul
My grace

I wandered long
I wandered far
Each day I woke
I cursed, I swore

Why must I live?
Why must I feel?
This endless pain
This life surreal

Each day's the same, the tears, the pain
I beg, I plead for some relief
It comes at times
It's always brief

I creep, I crawl
Upon my knees
Begging
For relief, release

Why, I ask
Must this be so?
The answer comes
It is 'no'

No, I say
What does that mean?
That's not an answer
This is a dream

The voice speaks softly
Yet profound
The pain will leave in the moment
I choose to cease my inner torment

The sadness exceeds its time and place
Only because I reject the grace
That's within my heart
And on the face

Of all the children
On this earth
Who suffered loss
Who suffered hurt

I open my heart
I open my eyes
I feel, I see that love resides
In everything and everyone

As I open to this love
It gently touches my broken heart
Creates a place
From which I start

To see the world
In a different way
Not so dark
Not so grey

I see the flowers as they bloom
I hear the birds sing a tune
I feel the sun's warmth upon my face
I hold a baby and feel God's grace

6 august 2008

I have recently returned from vacation. This was the first time I have had a few days to do something besides work. While it was exhausting in many ways, it was also a wonderful time spent with Ann-Sofie, my dear friend from Sweden, and my daughter. We had activities in Dallas, Austin and Bryan/College Station filled with laughter and joy. Making the trip to Austin was difficult, however.

Several times I was drawn to visit the accident site and re-live my grief. I consciously chose not to do this, as I wanted to ensure Ann-Sofie had a great time in her first visit to the US. I purposely stayed in south Austin, my old stomping ground, in the hopes that I could separate the Austin that I knew and loved, from the Austin that forever took away my son. It is, in effect, an anomaly. Austin was my happy place.

Prior to living in Boulder and Stockholm, it was the city that won my heart and provided many wonderful experiences. I loved the hill country and spent hours running around Town Lake. Tyrell and I shared a love for Austin and this was the place that he chose to begin his life once he was discharged from the Marines. His goal was to be living in Austin on 1 December and we were slightly delayed and he moved to Austin on 19 December.

I wish that I had the capacity . . . or ability . . . to hold fast to our common love of Austin and continue to enjoy this beautiful city. However, at this time, I only feel betrayal for the city that once held my adoration.

This evening was the first day in 3 days that I have taken a shower, or left the house. I have this love/hate relationship with my job. On the one hand, I am grateful, especially at this time, to be able to work from home and expend what little energy I have in areas other than getting ready for work and then driving to work.

On the other hand, I have found that I abuse this freedom with abandon. It is not uncommon for me to stay within my house, venturing no further than my porch, for days at a time. At least that has been my experience since February.

In the beginning I simply had enough energy to work, and that was it. Walking into my office and sitting at my computer for 9 hours a day, five days a week, was a monumental task and I felt a small bit of accomplishment upon the completion of each day.

Working from my home also offered me tremendous latitude in the grieving process. As long as I was not on a conference call, I could open myself to the grief bursts, as they appeared, and allow myself some time to let the river of tears perform their cleansing work. As painful as it is to grieve, not allowing oneself to grieve is even more painful, as the amount of energy required to live in denial is significant.

It was my bereavement counseling session this evening that got me in the shower and out of the house. I also had my monthly cranial sacral session right after counseling. Both of these activities have been instrumental to my healing process and I am deeply grateful.

14 august 2008

Today I hit the wall. By the time that I completed work it was close to 8:00p and I was at a point of physical and mental exhaustion. Somehow, and at some point in time, I lost myself again at work. Interesting word 'lost'. It implies that I don't know where I am . . . or I cannot find myself . . . and that is not entirely accurate. In actuality I have systematically adjusted my boundaries to where I was without any defenses and became so *wrapped* up in the job that I forgot to take care of myself.

This has been an ongoing challenge my entire career. I had thought, however, that I had learned my lesson in Sweden and would fulfill my commitment to myself of not going *back* to that way of working once I returned to the States. In fairness to me, it wasn't intentional. I wasn't throwing myself into my work to *forget* what happened. It was more akin to being on automatic and just doing what was in front of me and doing my best to keep putting one foot in front of the other.

As is often the case, however, the results are the same regardless of the intent. So here I am, once again, wondering what to do next. I feel as if I have the flu and decide to go to bed and simply rest. As no decision must be made today, tomorrow offers a new day and, perhaps, a new perspective.

15 august 2008

I slept poorly last night, and awoke hourly throughout the night. My mind appears to be manically grasping for a solution when it isn't even sure what the question is. I drag myself into my office and turn on the computer. The first thing is to view my calendar and see what meetings are mandatory and what meetings can be rescheduled.

I determine that two meetings must be held and reschedule the remaining meeting listed. I send an urgent mail to my PMA and ask if she can attend the meetings and take care of any situations that arise which cannot wait until Monday, and to give me a call on my mobile. Nearly two hours later I receive a call and she agrees to take the meetings and will stand in as my backup. I send an out of office mail and go back to bed.

Sleep, however, eludes me. I walk to the kitchen and grab several tablets of Vitamin C and Echinacea to boost my immune system. It isn't a quick fix, however, it makes me feel better. I go to my work computer to check mail my email, however, the screen is blank. I reboot my machine and the screen stays lit for a few minutes and then blanks again. Unbelievable, I say to myself.

This is exactly the same thing that happened 5 months ago and I know the only solution is to call Hardware Support. I make the call and explain the situation. They inform me that a shell will be shipped tomorrow. Will it arrive before 10:00a? I have a haircut scheduled and I have already gone way past the allotted time and I am suffering with my bangs poking my eyes at the most inconvenient times. I am informed that the time cannot be guaranteed and I resolve to the fact that I will have to reschedule my appointment.

I take a moment to reflect that while I have so few events that take place outside work, it is amazing how many times I cancel or reschedule personal appointments. It certainly is something that begs more attention and thought, however, now is not the time. I determine that while I acknowledged that I needed a rest, since I obviously do not have the conviction to take the 'day off', the universe is telling me that it will assist me. The thought brings a small smile to my face as I think "what now?"

I receive an email from Sheri Soltes telling me that we are within $800 of raising the $10,000. I am elated and I pick up the phone to call her. She mentioned that she was just getting ready to contact me because the total that she provided was inaccurate. We are actually at $9,000 and they are waiting for the matching grant from my company.

Quick math tells me I am $500 away from my goal. I tell Sheri that I will send the money after I speak with the family. I chat with Sheri a few more minutes as it is always a pleasure to talk with her. She is such a positive person and her 'realness' is refreshing. She asks me what I am going to do the remainder of the day and I tell her the only plans I have is to get a pedicure. One of the few things that I do for myself that is purely and absolutely unnecessary. No one 'needs' a pedicure, which makes receiving one so wonderful because I actually feel I am giving myself a gift.

After I hang up the phone I decide that the $500 will come from Tyrell's estate. It seems fitting that the remaining funds required comes from him. This is one of the benefits of being the Administrator and beneficiary as well; I get to make these unilateral decisions. I am thrilled to be writing the check and actually feel my energy level increasing. Having something positive to focus on has done wonders for my mental state. I am still having mild flu-type-symptoms however the heaviness appears to be dissipating.

I reflect on my conversation with Sheri and start thinking of names for the dog. It is exciting to be able to name the dog in memory of Tyrell. My first inclination is to wait until the dog is identified and let the dog 'provide' the name. My daughter has a different approach. She supports Sheri's position and wants to come up with a name. And to counteract my position of *we do not know the sex of the dog*, she states that we will have boy and girl names. The whole process reminds me of when I was pregnant with the children and how thrilling it was to pick out names. I concede to the approach and begin to consider names.

As I am thinking of names, I recall the discussion Sheri and I were having regarding recipients. She had relayed all of the steps that the organization has taken to *get the word out* and they are still challenged to locate the people who have the need. I begin to ponder possibilities of how I can help and become excited as I rush to take a shower and dress. I now know what I am going to do this afternoon.

My first stop is the VFW Post in Bryan. I walk into the building and ask to speak with someone in charge. A gentleman listens to my request and dials a number. He then briefly explains my request and hands me the phone. As it turns out I am speaking with the man who has been a member for 20 plus years and is involved at a state level.

He was very gracious and asked that I leave any information that I have and he will pick it up later that evening. He promised to communicate the information to the other Posts and thanked me for stopping by. I felt tears forming in my eyes as I hung up the phone and handed the papers to my contact and asked him to make copies. As I left I felt tremendous gratitude and began thinking about my next stop.

The Marines have an officer training office located in one of the local bank buildings. I drive to the building and begin ascending the steps. As I approach the door I notice the sign. They are closed for the week and will not return until the following Monday. As I step away I notice Congressman Edwards' office is next door. Congressman Edwards is a strong supporter of the Marines and I consider stopping by and asking for his help. I decide against it and walk to my car as I decide where I will go next.

I decide I will stop by the VA Counseling facility in College Station. Cynthia was extremely helpful and supportive when I met her shortly after Tyrell was killed. As I am driving to the office I feel hopeful. I enter the building and sign-in. Twenty minutes later a counselor calls my name and I walk to his office. I begin to tell him my story and he tells me that he cannot help me.

He noticed that Tyrell was a Marine and he suggests that I contact the Marine Corps League and provides me with two phone numbers.

DAYTON WILLIAMS

They have a Program called Marines Helping Marines and they would have more direct contact with the Marines in need. I thank him and as I am leaving I consider my next stop.

I determine that the media is a powerful tool, and I have a strong need. I drive to the Bryan-College Station Eagle, the local newspaper, and ask to speak with someone regarding a human interest story. I tell my story again, cognizant of the fact that I need to keep it as short as possible. The lady picks up her phone and places a call asking the person if they have a few minutes to speak with me. I follow the gentleman into a conference room and begin to tell my story again.

I explain that I have raised the money, however, a recipient has not been identified. I ask for their assistance in *getting the word out.* It is almost like selling in that it's a numbers game. The more contacts one makes, the more likely they will identify a potential buyer. The gentleman promises to submit the story to his editor and see if they are able to run the story. Once again I hand over my stack of papers to be copied. We shake hands and I leave the building. As I walk to my car I glance at my watch and it is only 4:15p. I have time for one more stop.

I make my way back to Congressman Edward's office. Not surprisingly the congressman wasn't in however his admin was very accommodating and took all of my papers to make copies. I told her that I had no idea how the congressman could help, but anything is possible. I ask her if she is willing to make an extra copy for the Marines and give it to them when they return next week. "Of course, I would be happy to" she replies.

As I am preparing to leave I look into her eyes and I see the tears forming. She reaches across her desk and gives me a hug and tells me that she is a mom, too. I am so touched by her compassion that I accept the hug with gratitude. As I leave the office I have the strong sensation that something will germinate from the seeds planted today. It is only a matter of time. As I reach my car, I decide it is now time to get my pedicure and use the next hour to simply relax.

29 august 2008

I define me. While this statement represents a core belief, I have discovered that I have misplaced not only my beliefs, but my understanding of who I am. A tragedy will do that. It is not so much a conscious decision as it is a byproduct of the confusion that has overtaken the mind and spirit. It is as if the mind determines how much 'stress' one can take and it erects a shield of protectiveness. The effect is two-fold however. While it may offer a protection from the grief by allowing it to penetrate in small doses, it also disengages one from self. It is as if a fog has permeated the mind body and spirit and we are required to relearn how to function.

The feeling compares with what I experienced as a young teenager. Often I was insecure which perpetuated my isolation from the world. During these past few months I have spent a great deal of time in isolation and found it difficult to perform simple things, e.g. grocery shopping.

In fact, anything that required interaction with mass numbers produced sensory overload followed by a rapid retreat back into my protective shell. If I stopped and *witnessed* how I was feeling, it was if I was someone else; or, at the very least, someone that I was more than 20 years ago. The impact to my psyche was overwhelming as not only did I not recognize myself, I did not know what *to do* to regain myself.

This evening my daughter and I did another 30 minute walk on our respective treadmills. As we are walking and talking, I express something that has been bothering me for some time; I feel disgust from my children and it pains me deeply. My daughter responds with the comment that it is not disgust, it is frustration mixed with concern. While I express appreciation for the honesty and the feedback, I also have a sensation of being cut at my core. How can my children be frustrated with me? They, more than anyone, understand what I have gone through as they have experienced it themselves.

As I feel the sensation of flight swell within me, I breathe deeply to calm myself so that we can continue to talk. My daughter's perspective is this is temporary, and it will pass. I, however, feel the damage has been done and I will never be able to regain what I had with my children. Feelings, however, do not necessarily reflect reality . . . they merely reflect the perspective at the moment. Scolding them, chiding them or ignoring them do not serve any purpose. My only objective is to embrace them and as I acknowledge them, I take the first step to freedom. The step, however, is taken again and again and again. My movement through grief has been 5 steps back for every 2 steps forward.

30 august 2008

The story was published in the Bryan/College Station Eagle today. I have been preoccupied with the publication as I was concerned the focus was misdirected from my purpose. Once I awoke and dressed, I went to the local Chevron station and bought 8 copies. As I sat down with my coffee and opened the paper, I found myself holding my breath.

I reminded myself, again, that if the story helps to get the word out, and a recipient is located, the mission was accomplished. The focus is not on what is said; it is on what outcome it produces. I then begin to read the story and find my eyes filling with tears as I take a moment to experience the grief again and acknowledge that I miss my son. I complete the story and begin again. I read it 4 times before I set it aside. Some of the information was inaccurate, and I do not believe the focus was in highlighting the need of a recipient. Nevertheless, the story has been told and I have fulfilled my part at this time.

I sit and ponder my conversation yesterday with the woman from the Foreign Legion. Her young son returned from Iraq physically whole, however, his spirit has been deeply wounded with post-traumatic stress. As I listened to her story, my heart ached for I understand her pain. Her son is with her, yet he isn't fully present. His pain is so great that it impacts his ability to function as a husband, father, son, friend . . . as a man. I empathize with this type of pain for I have spent over 20 years healing from my own personal pain and traumas that defined my life prior to the loss of my son.

As I reflect her story, I begin to relate this young man's story with all of humanity. There is pain all around us. Every person we meet has a story, and a journey that they must take. The stories are different however, the journey is the same: how do we awaken to our true selves? How to we embrace the situations that enter our lives and allow them to expand us as human beings as opposed to destroying us? As I ponder these questions, I ask myself: How can I participate in the healing of others? Is that my next purpose, and how am I to accomplish this?

The answers have not yet materialized however the thoughts have served their purpose. As the planting of a seed allows for the creation of a plant, the planting of a thought allows for the creation of a life changing event. As I open myself to the possibilities, I affirm my desire to fulfill my purpose in this life. What will unfold next?

31 august 2008

I watched two movies today: Home of the Brave and Apocalypto. The subject matter evoked tremendous emotions that have left me exhausted. Both of them deal with war and the impact on the souls of those who survive. Each movie represents the journey that an individual takes when confronted with horror and trauma beyond the norm of everyday life.

The impact to the individual varies according to their interpretations and perceptions of the event. As I was watching the drama unfold before me, I realized that our psyches do not distinguish between events nor do they place a number on a scale as to the impact, i.e 1-10. A tragedy, regardless of how it happens or to whom it happens to, requires the same steps to healing. Consequently each person must process the event and come to a place of acceptance in order to be restored to ease.

As I processed the complexity and enormity of this thought, I became acutely aware of the tremendous amount of emotional pain in our world. It was staggering and overwhelming at the same time! I wondered how this can possibly be.

If all of us are suffering, in some form or fashion, it would seem that we all have a tremendous amount of love and compassion for our fellow human beings. Yet, the opposite appears to be true. We are not only oblivious to the pain in others, most are oblivious to the pain within. We are asleep and walk through our lives as if we are in a dream; always the observer and never the participant. I weep for all humanity. Is it possible that I can not only heal myself but have an impact on the healing of others? I am daunted by the question and wonder if I have the courage to seek an answer.

Trauma changes a person. It is inevitable. What makes the same scenario affect people differently? The obvious answer is there are multiple variables involved and, therefore, it is impossible to say that everyone experienced the 'exact' situation. The obvious aside, the question still remains.

At a minimum, it is how the person perceives the event that affects how they respond to the event. After experiencing my personal tragedy, I found that my beliefs were dramatically challenged. While I have a strong foundational belief that *everything happens for a reason,* the emotional impact was still significant because there were so many other events on the periphery that I was assaulted from every direction.

I suspect this is very much what happens to all of us and part of the bereavement process is to redefine ourselves along the way. We know that we will be forever changed because of the event, however, what does that change *look like?* And to what degree does it change us?

3 january 2009

It has been some time since I have written. I have mentally listed several reasons, however, there really is only one reason; it is painful to write. The journey of grief takes a tremendous toll on one's psyche; it requires a significant amount of energy.

Writing, for me, has always been a healing exercise. It allows a vehicle of expression that supports problem solving. However, the day-to-day activities of life, dispersed with moments of grief, leaves little room for the soul searching usually accomplished through journaling. I have a limited amount of energy and I chose to put my energies in the here and now; confident that I would once again begin to capture and explore my thoughts through writing. The time has come.

Patience is a form of action. I recently read those words and wished that I had captured where I read it and who to attribute these profound words to. They eloquently spoke to me because this past year has presented so many challenges that often the only thing that I could do was to just be patient. In the beginning I cried often and with intensity. Although after several months the intensity and duration decreased, I wondered if it would ever end.

This was an instance where patience was the action I took. I promised myself that I would commit a year to my healing and allow myself to feel anything and everything that sprang forth. There were many times that I viewed my commitment to be bolder than I had the capacity to uphold; I could not endure crying one more day. Nevertheless, both my commitment and my patience supported my progress; even though the progress was rocky at best.

I can be thankful for the many life experiences I encountered that sustained me during my journey. For example, along the way I relearned that stuffing my feelings deep within my soul was counterproductive to a healthy body, mind and spirit. Consequently, I chose to feel each and every emotion that presented itself to me. Since thoughts result from emotions, and I am a deep thinker, I was continuously bombarded with emotions. For good or ill, I had lots of opportunities to practice fulfilling my commitment. At this time, I can gratefully say that my efforts were not in vain.

I scheduled vacation from noon 24 December until 5 January. I was completely unavailable for work.

7 june 2009

I am antsy. It has been over 15 months since Tyrell's death and I am still living in Bryan and I still do not know what I am doing with my life. Caleb has proposed to Hope and I have a strong feeling that they will marry in August. My thoughts of moving to Juneau have fizzled and I have been waiting to hear from Australia regarding a position that I applied for. My thoughts have centered on leaving the country and getting as far away as possible. Australia would accomplish that goal.

The previous Sunday morning I had the thought that if I cannot get to Australia through my present employer, then I will seek another way. I go to the Australia immigration site and fill out the form . . . which is quite lengthy . . . and receive a message. To paraphrase it says something about thanking me for my interest, however, I do not have enough points to be considered for entry. How can that be? I am a highly successful professional and feel slighted that Australia does not value my potential contributions.

I decide to go to the section that lists the professions that Australia deems important and review their associated 'points'. I am reading down through the list and see mid-wife. I stop, sit back in my chair, and hear the sound *humph* escaping from my lips. When the children were young, I had daydreamed of becoming a mid-wife. I now have a mission.

Researching nursing schools and midwifery schools across the United States consumed the entire day. I finalize on three schools and submit requests for additional information. It is now late in the evening and I rise from my chair and have this sense of energy emitting from me in all directions. I feel refreshed and motivated as I now have a plan to pursue.

The school that is most aligned with my goal is the University of Texas in Austin. I spent a week trying to convince myself that I could live in Austin to accomplish my goal. However, I encountered roadblocks in every direction. I learned long ago that if something is meant to be it does not have to be forced. And I could acknowledge that I was forcing this to work out simply because I wanted to leave Bryan so desperately. I went back to researching and discovered University of Texas Medical Branch in Galveston. While it did not have a midwifery program, it did offer an accelerated BSN program and I would then have the opportunity to get a master's afterwards. I now have a new direction. I am moving to Galveston.

To accomplish great things, we must not only act, but also dream, not only plan, but also believe.
—Anatole France

LaVergne, TN USA
12 August 2010
193115LV00005B/214/P